God's Image in Man

by

Henry Wood

Contents

I. The Nature of God.

"From Thee, great God, we spring, to Thee we tend,
Path, Motive, Guide, Original, and End."

WHAT AN overwhelming subject for contemplation! Can the human interpret the Divine? Philosophers have reasoned about it, poets have sung of it, mystics have dreamed of it, and prophets, apostles, and martyrs have had it revealed to them in varying degrees of distinctness. Let us in the simple character of dear children, yearning to know more of Our Heavenly Father, confidingly draw near to Him. The feebleness of our loftiest perception inclines us to shrink back, when we would come face to face with the Infinite. We are confronted by our materialism, our spiritual dulness, the magnitude of the subject, and the poverty of language and expression. Solomon's Temple could not contain Him, and so our most expanded and enlightened comprehension is too puny to hold more than a few drops from the Ocean of Infinity. As we humbly and reverently come into the presence of the "Consuming Fire," let us put off the shoes of our materiality, for we are upon holy ground.

And yet, with all our littleness and ignorance, we receive a warm welcome to the Divine Banquet. As thoughts of the Eternal Mind, and as sparks from that Spiritual Flame which energizes the created universe, we turn lovingly to our Great Source.

In time past we lingered outside the GREAT TEMPLE; we studied its façade from different standpoints; we were curious about the order and symmetry of its architecture; we surveyed its lintels and door-posts, and admired their delicate carvings and tracery. If we stepped over the threshold, we employed ourselves in the outer vestibule with the dutiful observance of ordinances, sacraments, rituals, and penances. We lingered before tablets, dusty with age, trying to decipher their inscriptions of arrested developments of truth, cast into the hard outline of formulated creeds and confessions. The draperies which separate the vestibule from the Great Auditorium were drawn close by the invisible wires of literalism, materialism, and sectarian loyalty. Let us not longer remain outside among symbols and shadows, but with joyful hearts accept the eternal invitation to come in, and surround ourselves with the endless profusion of good things in the Kingdom of the Real.

Our highest concept of the One Universal Power, Life, Intelligence and Will, we call God. Other nations and peoples have designated their supreme ideals of the Infinite, as Jehovah, Buddha, Allah, the Great Spirit, and many other names, in the vain attempt to adequately express Him through the feeble power of language. The word God originally meant Good. Various suggestive definitions have been given to his name as aids in perfecting our conception of Him. He is infinite Love, Wisdom, Goodness; and there is no space, place, time, state, nor condition where He does not live and express Himself. To Him nothing can be added, and from Him nothing can be taken away. The divine life is also manifested to us in Order, Law, Harmony, Peace, Wholeness, Truth, Intelligence, Beauty, and Happiness. Our Heavenly Father is perhaps the fittest appellation to apply to that superlative mental picture which is our representation of Him to our own consciousness.

But in glancing backward through the ages and around us at the present time, we find Him designated by other titles which are misleading. He has been called Lord, Sovereign, King, Ruler, Judge, and Potentate. In a certain sense He is all of these; but their primary and peculiar meanings have come from the manifested characters of ambitious and erring men who have assumed these offices. As applied, they have humanized God instead of deifying man. The King was not God-like, but God was made King-like. Fatherhood and Kingship are almost at antipodes. The former signifies love, care, mercy, discipline, tenderness, sympathy; the latter is a synonyme for pride, ambition, haughtiness, inaccessability, and severity. Cæsarism and imperialism stamped their impress upon titles and governments long before there was any general idea of human brotherhood or of republican institutions, and their dark shadows covered mediæval theology. Kingship is arbitrary and artificial, while fatherhood is natural. The word Sovereign as applied to God is not found in the Bible, and yet sovereignty is the emphasized centre of Calvinistic theology.

Influenced by the corrupt association of titles and false theological conceptions, a distorted view of God has long prevailed in the minds of men. Even the very terms used to distinguish Him, lent their associations to degrade his character. The haughtiness and tyranny which characterized Oriental despots were such important elements in all government, that their false analogies colored all the theology of the early church fathers. Calvin and Luther were also dominated by it, and still later the prevailing current of thought expressed by Jonathan Edwards was Divine Sovereignty as manifested in unconditional Force and Will. By contrast, how natural, lovable, and father-like are the New Testament delineations of God. How the utterances of Jesus and the writings of the beloved disciple glow with warmth and tenderness in their portraiture of the divine nature!

It has often been demonstrated that man's mental and even physical well-being has vital relations with his concept of God. This is an old truth (all truth is eternal), but our recognition of it needs to be awakened. The most impartial and scientific research shows that a wholesome and normal apprehension of God distinctly tends to express itself in harmony and healthfulness of both mind and body. All spiritual quality finds manifestation. God includes all primary causation. All springs, roots, and causes ultimate in Him. Our so-called causation is generally secondary. The Scriptures are crowded with broad and practical promises which have lost their significance because of our gross materialism. Paul says, "Ye are [not shall be] complete in Him." But we have lost the consciousness of such completeness. A self-centered sense of sufficiency has taken its place, which brings forth the bitter fruit of incompleteness. Internal conditions translate themselves outwardly. Such an order is logical and scientific. What external refreshment can be compared with the glorious sense of divine infoldment? What fair sunny clime or salubrious retreat can equal a dwelling in "the secret place of the Most High"? What strength like the "Strong Tower," and what defence like "His shield and buckler"? With David we can say: "He is the health of my countenance and my God." Weary, weak, and distressed brother or sister, hold in the inner chamber of your soul the healing thought: "In Him we live and move and have our being," and keep it there until its vivifying presence sends a glow through your whole being. Clasp it in your consciousness until you feel the divine heart-throbs pulsating through the channels of your entire complex nature.

Our trust in the breadth of the divine beneficence has been mainly theoretical, and therefore we have turned to external systems instead of the Overflowing Fountain. God is our life, and it is only when the conduits which connect us with Him are obstructed, that we are conscious of dryness and leanness. If we "abide under the shadow of the Almighty," His glorious wholeness will impress its influence upon both soul and body. Thought has a wonderful moulding power. "As a man thinketh, so is he." Thought of the Living One, and of His image in us, vitalizes the unseen springs of our being, even down to the subsoil of its physical basis.

When we gaze God-ward our vision is so colored by subjective states, that the Unchangeable wears the aspect of mutability. He is something different to us to-day from what He was at any time in the past. Different observers see Him in the various aspects of Justice, Love, Anger, Mercy, Power, Goodness, Severity, Wrath, Sovereignty, Harmony, Cruelty, Law, and even as Blind Force. The idea of God is unique in respect to the great diversity of its qualities to men. Any name, even that of God, is only the outward label for a mental image. When it is presented to the eye or ear, it calls up a mental delineation which has real existence in us, whether correct or deformed.

To the ancient Israelites God was a tribal or a national Deity, and even a Military Leader. He fought their battles, and when angry He was propitiated by burnt offerings and sacrifices. But with all their misconceptions, their monotheism exalted them far above the surrounding polytheistic nations. After centuries of slow progress their idea of God became broadened and spiritualized, and in the period of the primitive church, reached its highest development. But a little later a strange reactionary movement set in towards anthropomorphism. After the Apostolic period the materialistic concept of God soon became prevalent, and colored prevailing theologies; and even in this nineteenth century, its cold, mechanical limitations are only slowly fading. A humanized Deity, having a localized habitation, and possessing parts and passions, lingers with great pertinacity in the minds of men. When our standpoint is located below the white light of the spiritual horizon, a distorted God is visible. The material man sees Him as an infinitely magnified image of the human self. Man's unworthy motives, opinions, and ideas of justice, as though seen through a great telescope, are clothed with divine outlines and proportions. The vindictive man worships a vindictive God. The austere, selfish morality of the "elder brother" is often associated with the divine character. Besides these self-reflected false images of God, systems of theology have painted many unlovable views of Him, and men are repelled by their hard outlines. Towards any true divine concept, humanity is drawn naturally and unconsciously. Man feels the link which binds him to God so distinctly that atheism would be almost impossible, were it not that a falsity has been set up and called God. Scholastic theology has represented

Him as an august Monarch, seated upon a great throne, who glories in his sovereignty and imperialism. It has made his character autocratic and wrathful, and the natural outcome has been a formal worship inspired by fear and dread. Conscious of his weakness and sin, man cringes before God as an offended, omnipotent Personality, instead of seeking Him for strength and succor. Not wishing to bring God into his own guilty consciousness, so far as possible he has kept the "Present Help" out of his thoughts. The human elements in the Old Testament Scriptures are filled with perverted ideals of God, which have the qualities of men, and these were re-enforced by the traditions and interpretations of mediæval theology.

Oh, broken and bruised humanity! how have you suffered and agonized as you looked up to such a God!

Oh, weak and timorous children of men! bound in iron fetters, how have you trembled as such a nightmare overshadowed you!

What floods of tears have expressed the desolation and helplessness of stricken souls who had only a caricature of God placed before them!

How the love-tendrils from infantile and childish hearts, spontaneously thrust out to "feel after Him," have been chilled and paralyzed!

Thank Heaven, such monstrous perversions belong mainly to the past, and golden rifts are now everywhere seen in the clouds which for so long were impenetrable. By filling humanity with a slavish fear of God, designing men more effectively promoted their monarchical and ecclesiastical dominion. It has been a moral impossibility for the human heart to "pant after" Him when presented in such false proportions.

God cannot be seen through the intellect. Dogmatism has built up a logical and institutional Deity, and though he be moral and lawful, he is not lovable. In order to kindle love in the breast of man, he must behold that which in its own nature is attractive. The scholastic conceptions of God have been so sharply drawn, that they amount to a mental graven image. There is a world-wide chasm between a spiritual perception of God, and the very best concept which can be formed by intellectual processes. The one sees and feels the Eternal Life, Love, and Truth, while the other theorizes upon a legal or mechanical force, as an objective Deity. The first glows in the depths of its own being with reflected warmth and brightness, while the last is a frame-work of system, fitted together by scholastic logic. The unaided intellect is color-blind to divine harmony.

Idolatry was never more prevalent than at the present time. It is only when the gods of worldly ambition, of mammon, of fleshly appetites, of the baser self and the material body, are hurled from their pedestals, that our clarified vision begins to discern the Eternal One. We also pay unconscious homage to modern, material invention and scientific achievement. We are looking forward to some Golden Age which will be ushered in by a new social order; nationalized land, impossible poverty, perfected legislation, improved medication, sanitation and communication. When these external ideals occupy the thought, and form the great desideratum, they become idols. The belief that mankind can realize completeness and happiness in these achievements, rather than in God, amounts to an idolatrous homage. How ever desirable, they are secondary.

How often the crudity of our childish ideas clothed God with material form and gigantic human outline, and such imagery is still present in some degree in many adult and even scholarly minds. If the spoken name of the Deity brings before the mind any image having material quality, it is a graven image, and therefore an "other" god than the One who is Spirit. The gross ideals of the mediæval church, and also those of later periods, were grotesquely expressed by the old masters, who represented the Father as an aged man, with flowing hair and beard, and stern, dignified bearing.

Anthropomorphism has insisted upon the conception of God as a person. In a sense we may call Him personal, and yet the term, to most minds, conveys the idea of limitation. To whatever degree our concept of Him involves such a quality, it is false, and therefore idolatrous. How impotent is human language for the expression of Divinity! Its narrow definitions do not fit the Infinite. Beware, Beloved, lest we hastily call our brother an atheist or a pantheist, because his idea of God does not quite coincide with ours. Of the two, his concept may be the truer and larger. The Infinite Love, Life, Will, and Intelligence, is the true God. Unless the term person is enlarged and lifted infinitely above that which it signifies to most minds, it is too circumscribed to define the All in All. Any mental image of God which has to do with changeableness or with any materialistic form, locality, height, breadth, or depth, is false, and with a wrong beginning every logical outcome will be perverted.

All true religion must have for its basis a right conception of God. This is at once the centre and foundation. If the starting-point be wrong, the problem of man's relation to his Maker will not be solved. It has been said: "If man has a false idea of God, his love of God is the love of an untruth, and everything will be in some degree wrong with him." Friends, ponder the tremendous import of such a fact. How full is the world and the church of unconscious idolatry! In a certain sense man creates the God he worships. His own mental concept receives his homage, and it is in some degree of his own construction. The Calvinist has formed a different idea of God from the Arminian, and the Trinitarian from the Unitarian. The tribal, the national, the traditional, the institutional, and the denominational deities have had human shading and coloring. All such concepts, and such as are peculiar to "Jerusalem" and "this mountain," need to be rectified by a worship which is consciously "in spirit and in truth." It is only as we go beneath "the letter" that we find the true spiritual idea of God delineated in the Bible, which portraiture also found concrete outward expression in the Christ. A correspondence of these ideals is also discovered in the intuitional deeps of our own souls, when we delve beneath the false strata of materialism and dogmatism. Intellectual tradition and speculation have veiled our spiritual eyes, and thus the likeness of God has become dimmed and humanized. Even by religious teachers, and in theological systems, God has been presented as the Author of evil, trouble, and disease, and as actively exercising the reflected human qualities of hate, wrath, and vengeance. At the same time, men have been told that they must love such a God *supremely* under the alternative of endless punishment. The choice thus presented has been either eternal woe, or a moral impossibility. Dogmatic systems have clothed God with a Roman sternness of legality and unapproachableness.

Oh, sincere but mistaken teachers, who have evolved such a Deity from your dark imaginings, and then expected that your brothers and sisters would yearn after him; go back, and with child-like humility learn the alphabet of His nature! Oh, desponding brother, to whom life is a "vale of tears," know that the dark universe upon which you gaze is but a reflection of your magnified selfish gloom! Oh, inwardly barren soul, be not surprised that God's green fields are, to you, a veritable Sahara! Oh, weary, footsore pilgrim on life's journey, with your field of vision filled with shadows and spectres, rise to a higher standpoint, and the Sun of righteousness will dissolve all clouds and illumine the whole horizon!

God is not a mixed being of opposite and conflicting principles, as good and evil, love and hate. Unity and harmony form his monogram which He has stamped upon the open page of nature, and graven upon the tablets of the hearts of his children.

We misunderstand God in what we call the "acts of his providence." There are certain orders of events which are entirely beyond human control, as earthquakes, tornadoes, and floods. There are others in which there is a seeming mixture of human and divine agency. Regarding the first, some interpret such phenomena as sent directly by God, and others, as the outcome of "laws of nature" which were first instituted by Him, but which often prove terribly calamitous to man. An earthquake destroys a city, and many human lives are lost. How can God, who is infinite and unmixed Love, cause or permit such a calamity? It is at once assumed that such an event is an intrinsic evil, and therefore, as God must be the author of it, that He sends evil. Evil is a moral subjective human quality. How can it come out of Infinite Good? To solve such a problem, we must take a broader view in the perspective of the Real. Let us open the eyes of our spiritual understanding and see if we cannot find some interpretation of such occurrences. God is spirit; and man, being made in God's image, is also spirit. The intrinsic man is spirit, even on the present plane. Therefore no physical "calamity" can touch so much as a "hair of his head." Man's body is not man; but he has lost the consciousness that he is spirit, here and now (however well he may know it theoretically), and therefore has lost the divine and only true standpoint. He has grown materialistic, and unconsciously identified the ego with his *body*, which only exists as a form of external expression. In proportion to man's materialism, physical disaster to him implies evil. Only spiritual vision can distinguish the true proportion of events. We therefore confidently accept the proposition that God is Good, and All is Good. As spiritual bodies (divine images), here and now, no material catastrophe can harm us. In nature all movements are good, for they are in accord with natural law and development, and these are beneficent. No objective evil can pierce to the real or spiritual self. It is the animal, or false self, which beholds images of evil. Can we live in the body and not be of the body? Just in that degree that we have a constant and ruling consciousness of our divine birthright. A minor order of events, such as personal misfortune and disease, also gain their sombre aspect from our homage to matter. With a ruling spiritual consciousness, disease would finally disappear, for inner health and harmony would have exact correspondence in outward expression. "A good tree cannot bring forth corrupt fruit."

It is only to our color-blind and inverted vision that there appears to be two great opposing principles at warfare in the Universe. With the telescope of spirit, which reveals all that is real, we may sweep the illimitable Cosmos, and find harmony without discord,—One Principle, One Good.

Is not, then, the material or the physical life of value? Yes, it is sacred as an expression of what is within it. Only when mistaken for the Reality, and thereby idolized, does it become discordant and tyrannical. Viewed as external manifestation, it grows beautiful, and also becomes harmonious with the environment of its own plane.

We are utterly unable to discern the true God objectively, until the subjective torch in our own souls has been lighted. Darkness within, directly reflects outer darkness. The beloved disciple says: "God is light, and in him is no darkness." Darkness in the spiritual as in the physical world is negation. Its delusive appearance of reality comes from idolizing unreality. To clarify our vision we must centre our pure desire and aspiration upon the Supreme Good, and *hold it there* until the surrounding negation fades out of view. When the sun rises, the moon and stars disappear. When God is beheld in his Allness, opposites vanish into their native oblivion. Then selfhood is put under foot, and we are filled with the "mind of Christ."

"Having promise of the life that now is." God is our life, though we feel vitality as if it were our own. All life is God manifested. When selfhood is our life-centre, our orbit is eccentric and confused. God is the Living One, comprising both centre and circumference. Spirit is eternal, and death non-existent except to the eye of sense. Death is the casting-off of a crude form of expression for one which is more perfect, and therefore it is not death, but fuller life. A sense of matter is decay. An homage of the unreal is idolatry. Such senses of false life must die, but souls live, because they are images of God. Spirit is indestructible.

The cry of the human soul after God, and its restlessness until it finds Him, is because of its intrinsic oneness with Him. God is the counterpart and complement of humanity. Man is like a discordant musical instrument until he comes into recognized unison with his Maker.

There is an aspect of God which presents him as a Trinity. The threefold nature, as seen by man, furnishes a fulcrum as an aid to the finite in comprehending the Infinite. It is impossible for sensuous man to interpret Spirit (God) except through divine manifestation. In Christ, God filled the human mould perfectly, and that demonstration was an expression of divinity to mankind on the human plane. The Holy Spirit, as God, becomes a Guest of the human spirit, and thus a great seeming chasm between them is filled. God is one God, but to human view there is a threefold Deific demonstration. It is not God, composed of three distinct persons, but a triple manifestation of God to human consciousness, that constitutes the Trinity. To know God aright is "life eternal." To our rudimentary spiritual vision the Incomprehensible One is resolved. Our eyes would be blinded by the full effulgence of the white light of One Spirit and Life, and so it comes to us softened, divided, and expressed.

And yet. Beloved, God is not complex, and to know him, a child-like transparency is requisite, while the mightiest intellect may cry: "Oh, that I might find him!" A view from the top of the loftiest tower which can be built upon the intellectual plane, will not bring Him within the field of vision; but at the centre of every soul there is a "Mount of Transfiguration," from the summit of which we may get veritable glimpses of the Beautiful Reality. In the clear azure spanning that "Mount" we read a Name in letters of light, and that Name is LOVE.

II. Revelation Through Nature.

"Earth's crammed with heaven,
And every common bush afire with God:
But only he who sees, takes off his shoes."

THE KINGDOM of Nature intermingles with the Kingdom of Spirit. Each is the complement of the other, and no arbitrary boundary exists between them. Truth is a rounded unit. Any distortion or suppression of it, however narrowly localized, involves general loss. The scientist, while studying forms and laws, may be color-blind to the presence of an infinite spiritual dominion. If he dissociates Nature from her vital relations, his accomplishment can be but partial. So far as he fails to recognize her as a Theophany, he misses her true significance. Likewise the theologian, who has eyes only for the supernatural, fails to find the vital supports and relations of his own chosen realm. Each thereby makes his own system incomplete and untruthful. Nature and spirit can no more be divorced than a stream and its fountain. The attempt to translate Religion into an arbitrary, supernatural realm, has robbed it of its spontaneity and vitality. To the world the supernatural is unnatural, and the unnatural is morbid.

Spiritual vitality, like an over-flowing fountain, must outwardly manifest its exuberance. The natural type can only be interpreted as the divine type. When the veil of forms and chemistries is lifted, spiritual meanings are brought to light. Religion may be defined as natural unfoldment which brings into manifestation the divine type. The methods and transmutations of the natural world are a revelation of the Father. The spirit of Nature and the genius of the Gospel are in perfect accord because they have the same source. A spiritual interpretation is the only key which can unlock the motives and mysteries of cosmic forces, and reveal the rhythmical order of their operations. The lover of Nature will persistently follow her through outward shapings and phenomena, until her harmonies become audible. Such a pursuit takes us beyond the realm of shadows and illusions, and brings us face to face with idealistic Realism.

Whatever is abnormal generates unwholesome pessimism, and clouds the human horizon. The mere developments of material science cannot lighten the load of human woe, nor satisfy the cravings of man's spiritual being. The incubus of Artificialism is upon literature, society, and institutions. A debasing so-called realism in fiction and real life perpetuates its quality by what it feeds upon. Even education, in its ordinary sense, is powerless to raise men above the plane of shadows and illusions. When a false philosophy severs Nature from her vital relations, she becomes coldly mechanical and even adverse. Unrecognized as a process of divine evolution, she seems unfriendly and often vindictive. The friction, which, if rightly interpreted, would turn man back into a path of restoration, becomes so galling that—with its purpose lost sight of—it materializes into features of Satanic malignity. The subtle refinements which allure us away from the natural type, end in a chaotic degeneration. In the degree that institutions and systems take on abnormal shapes, they court decay. Civilizations, even when most distinguished for material progress and æsthetic culture, become top-heavy and fall because they lack a simple but true archetypal basis.

The term natural is sometimes used in a peculiar and degraded sense. St. Paul speaks of the natural man, meaning the baser and carnal selfhood, as distinguished from that which is higher and normal. But the former is the perverted and misshapen self; while the latter, after the divine type, is called "the temple of the Holy Ghost." To be spiritual is to be in the highest degree natural, and it is an abuse of language to use the two terms in antithesis.

He who sees God in Nature, feels the ecstatic thrill of the infinite Presence. The visible universe becomes to him a repository of mystery, harmony, and sanctity. This wholesome delight will all be missed by intellectual accomplishment if it be linked to a feeble spiritual intuition. A childlike soul which has no knowledge of Botany, but which is in touch with the Infinite, will find more in a flower than he whose technical but unsanctified understanding can fully define its laws and mechanism.

As our spiritual vision gains in acuteness, the objective universe grows more beautiful. A changed consciousness brings a new revelation of outward harmony and unity. God is the essence of Nature. We see him in the unfolding of the leaves, in every flower and blade of grass, in the air, the clouds, the sunshine, the sea. All are gilded and beautified. Each is a letter in the great open volume of the universe. As the sea contains all its waves, so the One Life embraces all lower forms of vitality. Such an interpretation is spiritual Theism, and has no alliance with Pantheism. Outward forms are beautiful in proportion as our consciousness grasps their plasticity to spiritual moulding.

"All are but parts of one stupendous whole,
Whose body nature is, and God the soul."

External nature is a grand panorama, unrolling day by day, and displaying marvellous beauty, color, and shape, painted by the Divine Artist for the enjoyment of his children. The universe is not soulless, but soulfull. Animate creation is a vast pastoral symphony, the delicious intonations of which can only be interpreted by the inner hearing. The sky, sea, forest, and mountain, are the visible draperies which, in graceful folds, thinly veil the Invisible One. As our physical organism is moulded and directed by the soul within, so is the whole creation permeated and vitalized by the Immanent God. When we study the rocks, plants, animals, man, if we delve deeply enough, we find the footprints of the unifying and energizing Presence. This is not merely poetic imagery, but scientific accuracy.

A recognition of the continual Deific manifestation thrills the human soul with joy and gladness. This, in itself, is evidence of its naturalness and truth. Nature is friendly. Her correspondences with man are so intimate and reciprocal that they demonstrate infinite wisdom, design, and unity. The barrenness and untruthfulness of Atheism are evident from their utter lack of power to arouse human responsiveness.

That vision is inspired which beholds mountains, forests, and rocks, as cathedrals and altars which enshrine the divine love and radiance. Every step we take is upon enchanted ground. By patient teachableness we realize not merely poetic beauty, but real truth, in the familiar lines:—

"Find tongues in trees, books in running brooks,
  Sermons in stones, and good in everything."

Their different interpretations of Nature, measurably determine the character of governmental systems, institutions, and literatures. Her function in shaping civilization, and giving expression to Art, is vital. The response of the intelligence and imagination of races and nations to her appeal, has determined their relative positions as factors in the world's progress.

Nature to the primitive Aryan was an inspiration, the vigor of which was long perceptible during his migrations and changing conditions. Arcadian simplicity always has been a saving force; an instinctive feeling after the divine type.

The Hebrew regarded Nature as the physical manifestation of the Deity, and looking behind external phenomena he found God. The poetry of Job brings to view some of the most vivid and sublime aspects of Nature—as a Theophany—that are found in any literature. The wonderful 104th Psalm is an inspired artistic picture of the universe, which interprets the profound intimacy with Nature which characterized the spirit of Hebrew psalmody.

"Who coverest thyself with light as with a garment: who stretchest out the heavens like a curtain:

"Who layeth the beams of his chambers in the waters: who maketh the clouds his chariot: who walketh upon the wings of the wind:

"Who maketh his angels spirits: his ministers a flaming fire:

"Who laid the foundations of the earth, that it should not be removed forever.

"Thou coveredst it with the deep as with a garment: the waters stood above the mountains.

"At thy rebuke they fled; at the voice of thy thunder they hasted away.

"They go up by the mountains; they go down by the valleys unto the place which thou hast founded for them.

"Thou hast set a bound that they may not pass over; that they turn not again to cover the earth.

"He sendeth the springs into the valleys, which run among the hills.

"They give drink to every beast of the field; the wild asses quench their thirst.

"By them shall the fowls of the heaven have their habitation, which sing among the branches.

"He watereth the hills from his chambers: the earth is satisfied with the fruit of thy works.

"He causeth the grass to grow for the cattle, and herb for the service of man: that he may bring forth food out of the earth;

"And wine that maketh glad the heart of man, and oil to make his face to shine, and bread which strengtheneth man's heart.

"The trees of the Lord are full of sap; the cedars of Lebanon, which he hath planted;

"Where the birds make their nests: as for the stork, the fir trees are her house."

. . . .

"O Lord, how manifold are thy works! in wisdom hast thou made them all: the earth is full of thy riches.

"So is this great and wide sea, wherein are things creeping innumerable, both small and great beasts."

"Thou crownest the year with thy goodness; and thy paths drop fatness.

"They drop upon the pastures of the wilderness: and the little hills rejoice on every side.

"The pastures are clothed with flocks; the valleys also are covered over with corn; they shout for joy, they also sing."

To the glowing vision of the Hebrew prophets. Nature was but a transparent medium through which they had a near view of the Infinite. The fervid imagery of Isaiah finds expression: "Break forth into singing, ye mountains, O forest and every tree therein." And again: "Sing, O heavens; and be joyful, oh earth;" thus making of all visible things a divine symphony.

But a tinge of anthropomorphism colors all the sacred Hebrew literature. God was viewed more as infinite physical Force than as infinite Spirit and Love. With an abundance of poetic and artistic symbolism, there is wanting that broader consciousness of divine harmony, adjustment, and beauty, with which a truer concept thrills the soul. The Hebrew saw Nature as moved upon by God, rather than as the constant radiant expression of divine life and unfoldment. Human fellowship with it, and translated goodness through it, are later and truer interpretations than those made by the Old Testament poets and prophets.

But what of modern materialistic views even less spiritual than those of the Hebrew? We find them limited to the scientific study of phenomena on the one side, or the æsthetic pleasure of form and color on the other. The significance and vitality of Nature are thereby lost. She is grasped by the intellect rather than enshrined in the heart. Art as an intellectual expression is cold and mechanical. The true artist must feel Nature as instinct with divine life, whether or not he be fully conscious of such an inspiration.

During the long gloomy period between the decay of classic culture and the Renaissance, inspiration through Nature almost ceased. The rigid austerity and asceticism which cast its shadow over the Middle Ages, obliterated the beauty and harmony of the visible creation. In such a light Nature appeared sickly, mechanical, and forbidding. Men found nothing attractive without, because they were conscious of no beauty within. Life became barren because Nature was barred out. Humanity was under a curse, and Nature shared in the disgrace. Men shut themselves up in cells, and lived behind bare walls, and put God's green fields out of their sight. Without the Immanent God, the visible universe was prosaic and stern, and its aspect would not have been improved even by the presence of a Deity who in Himself seemed unlovable.

When life loses its plasticity and grows conventional, it solidifies into unyielding forms, and religion becomes an institution, and worship a prescribed service in temples made with hands. The inner soulful interpretation of God is displaced by external definitions made by priestly orders and ecclesiastical authority. The outward sense is appealed to by imposing ceremonial, but the divine overflowing is lost amid the literal structure and dramatic ritual. Nature is persistent as a spiritual inspiration, but external noises prevent her low, sweet harmonies from being audible. Instead of letting her teach and lead us, we impose our intellectual interpretation upon her. She will not reveal her riches when pursued with gauges, measures, and microscopes, but will bestow her boundless wealth upon the patient seeker after truth, who comes into touch with her spirit.

We have elevated ranges of thought in our lives, which are like chains of material peaks as contrasted with the surrounding levels. "I will lift up mine eyes unto the hills from whence Cometh my help." We live too much on the lowlands of our natures. If we linger upon the hills of elevated thought, and dwell among the summits of spiritual aspiration, our lungs will become accustomed to their rare and pure atmosphere. We delve in the glens and caves, and then wonder that life is so cloudy, and our horizon so narrow.

The universe is a reflector of divine adornment, and is everywhere garnished with gems. We are invited to admire its beauty, inhale its fragrance, adore its symmetry and color, and through them to share in the depth and overflow of Deific goodness. Emerson says, "God has not made some beautiful things, but Beauty is the creator of the universe." Nature may always be trusted, for natural laws are divine methods. Each successive season is a benediction in changed form. When Spring awakens a quickening impulse of life, and bursts the bars of wintry frost, she transforms the face of Nature, and clothes it with a charm of fresh life and beauty. Every seed and bulb has within it a promise of the Resurrection. Every flower is a suggestion, and each unfolding leaf an expression of exuberant life, which everywhere manifests the divine redundancy. Nature's ministry soothes and heals human infelicities. She fits herself into man's angular spaces; smoothes and rounds out his broken and imperfect outlines, and like a grand orchestral accompaniment, supports and harmonizes his uncertain operations.

"To him who in the love of Nature holds
  Communion with her visible forms, she speaks
  A various language; for his gayer hours
  She has a voice of gladness, and a smile
  And eloquence of beauty; and she glides
  Into his darker musings with a mild
  And healing sympathy, that steals away
  Their sharpness ere he is aware."

What responsive soul can witness the splendor of a glorious sunset without being lifted out of the lower self, and inspired by its unearthly riches? Who can study the masses of fleecy cloud-forms, piled like Alps upon Alps, refulgent with the rays of the setting orb, and not feel a suggestion of the power by which the Sun of righteousness illumines the mists and fogs of man's deeper nature?

The purity of Nature appeals to all that is pure in humanity. She softens her angles, repairs her rents, carpets her bare spaces, covers her excrescences, and sweetens all taint and corruption. She embroiders her rocks with mosses and lichens, and her running brooks are crystalline in their purity until they are made turbid by man's artifice. Her chemistries rectify all decay, and transmute and sanctify all deformity. Her many voices in a diapason of praise are forever rendering tribute to their Author, and thereby interpreting His love and beneficence to the children of men. His constancy is typified by every blossoming rose, and every violet of the wood teaches a lesson of childlike trust and faith. The hills and mountains are symbols of His strength and majesty. He is the substance of all things.

"In Thee enfolded, gathered, comprehended,
  As holds the sea her waves—Thou hold'st us all."

The scale of Nature is infinite. When we attempt any intellectual solution of her mysteries, we are confronted by the fact that no absolute knowledge is possible, while of relative information we may build up a vast structure. The Absolute is wholly beyond reason and logic; but in the realm of spiritual perception, love, and goodness, we may know the Absolute, and become one with it. "Canst thou by searching find out God?" Through the intellect, never; but through the inner vision we may find Him. The intuitive perception is a natural perception, even though it be upon the spiritual plane. God, the Absolute, we may know through faith and love, and only through these and related unisons can we interpret the spirit of Nature. Her infinite scale as intellectually discerned—and man's limited place upon it— are vividly brought to light by late researches in physical science. Scientific authorities declare that the inexorable logic of the "relativity of knowledge" proves that in the actual (absolute) universe of being, there is neither time nor space, matter nor motion, form nor force, as we know them. Instead of matter as it appears, Modern Science insists that its phenomena are only explainable by the hypothesis of rhythm among attenuated atoms. No matter how compact a body may appear, chemistry and physics unite in affirming that its solidity is a mere illusion. Solid steel is composed of molecules that do not touch each other. These molecules are like a cloud of gnats, and appear as one because they move together. Solidity, like other material terms, only belongs to relative, sensuous, human consciousness, and does not touch absolute conditions. When rhythmical movements are favorable, bodies may pass through each other. Light passes freely through glass, and electricity through copper, though neither can force its way through a piece of wood, which is of much less density. The forces which keep material bodies in their form and being, in their final analysis are spiritual. The world of spirit fashions and supports the world of sense, and therefore the sensuous realm embraces only resultant phenomena. The world we see is a world of transitory illusions. To the degree in which our spiritual sight has been unfolded, we may penetrate beyond the shadows, and gain glimpses of the Real. We have never seen our friend, nor our very selves, but only manifestations and coverings. Gravitation may not be a spiritual power, but perhaps it is the link through which the spiritual domain rules and moulds the material. The reason why we see so little of the spiritual world through Nature, is because our spiritual faculties are but in an infantile stage of development. Even in physical existences, the range of our sensuous and intellectual consciousness is so limited, that, according to Modern Science, whole universes of beings may dwell among us or be passing through us, of whose presence we know nothing. Their colors, forms, and properties are so subtle, that only beings whose senses are far more acute than ours, can be introduced into their society. Weight, size, color, and form are nothing more than human subjective limitations. The discharge of a cannon makes no noise if there are no ears within range. It possesses a power to stimulate the listening ear, but the noise has no existence except in the hearing. There are forms of life below us which have but one, two, or three senses. Who can affirm that there are not other existences, invisible and unknown to us, who possess many more than five senses? An eminent scientist has recently made the startling suggestion, that not only below us may exist molecular universes, with orders, intelligences, and even civilizations, but that above us, perhaps, worlds may be but as molecules of grand universes, containing complex systems, organizations, and personalities. Such speculations in the realm of physical science have no value, unless, by the way of analogy, they may tend to quicken our apprehension of the spiritual verities, of which the material universe is but the letter upon the printed page. Oh, man, made in God's image, and linked to and nourished by Nature, what glorious opening vistas are before you in the eons of eternal progress!

Every atom and molecule, in all spaces and combinations, has its own peculiar rhythmical movement, and thus it joins in the universal anthem of praise to its Maker. All forms of life are registering their actions, and printing their biographies in the imperishable ether in which we dwell. The vibrations which we set in motion, go forth in indestructible strains, but a minute fraction of which, in passing, is momentarily caught by human ears. The late Professor Babbage, of England, in one of his treatises, compares the atmosphere to "a vast library, on the pages of which are registered unceasingly all that man has ever said, or woman whispered." Another gifted writer[1] concludes, "That there may be a world of spiritual existences around us,—inhabiting this same globe, enjoying the same nature,—of which we have no perception; that, in fact, the wonders of the New Jerusalem may be in our midst, and the songs of the angelic hosts filling the air with their celestial harmony, although unheard and unseen by us." Truly, "there are more things in heaven and earth than are dreamt of in our philosophy."

---

1. Professor J. P. Cooke in "Religion and Chemistry."

"Hearken! Hearken!
If thou would'st know the mystic song
Chanted when the sphere was young.
Aloft, abroad, the pæan swells;
O wise man! hear'st thou half it tells?
O wise man! hear'st thou the least part?
'Tis the chronicle of art.
To the open ear it sings,
Sweet the genesis of things,
Of tendency through endless ages,
Of star-dust, and star-pilgrimages.
Of rounded worlds, of space and time,
Of the old flood's subsiding slime.
Of chemic matter, force, and form,
Of poles and powers, cold, wet, and warm:
The rushing metamorphosis
Dissolving all that fixture is.
Melts things that be to things that seem,
And solid nature to a dream."

Nature is God translated into vitalized color, form, and beauty. The world is embellished by Spirit, and its inaudible testimony is the cadence of the gospel of love. Nature is a vast kindergarten, whose easy object-lessons train our childlike affections, so that they may gain strength to mount above and beyond. Her mountain-peaks of truth stand out sharp and clear above the fogs and mists of error. To view the Real, we must climb the mountainside, until our standpoint is above the leaden gloom of the lowland outlook.

We try to conform Nature to our notional concept of what she should be, instead of attending her school like willing pupils. We aim to shape her into correspondence with our selfish wills, instead of yielding our hardness to her graceful mould. Let us put our hand in hers, and thus hasten to gain her wholesome ministrations.

In Jesus, the Christ, was the supreme demonstration of the identity, in man, of the natural and spiritual type. His teaching was spontaneous and unconventional, and His education was not shaped by the formulas of the schools. In Him, that which had been buried in philosophies and hidden in institutions was brought to light, and interpreted to man upon his own plane. For the only time Humanity became perfectly transparent, so that the divine light and purity shone through it, unsullied and unperverted. He was the natural, the ideal, and the archetypal man. In Him the divine pattern of humanity was filled to the full. As Nature is a continuous divine manifestation, so Christianity is not limited to any age or dispensation. The historic Jesus was a temporary and material manifestation of the spiritual and eternal Christ. "That was the true Light which lighteth every man that cometh into the world." The typical man is spiritual and eternal because he is made in the Father's image. The essential Saviour is that manifestation of the love of God toward man, which is both natural and eternal. Sonship is neither fleshly nor limited. Christ as the ideal man was a prophecy, a first fruit. "The last Adam was made a quickening Spirit." The human embodiment of the Word was a manifested love without perversion, and was Nature's ultimate prototype.

III. Direct Revelation.

WE ARE living in a mortal dream. Our material environment appears to be substantial, but at intervals we are jostled and partially awakened from our sensuous vision. Our eyes are closed to the Real until something startles us, which, from its intensity, penetrates our consciousness, and discloses other relations and environments than those to which we have yielded our allegiance. Every man possesses a spiritual equipment; but if it has been hidden beneath the opaque shadows of material sense, so that its rightful owner is unaware of his glorious possession, to him it is as though it were not. Divine revelation signifies subjective spiritual unfoldment. It has been said that God is nearer to us than we are to ourselves; but if we are unconscious of the Presence, it has no meaning.

The method of spiritual revelation to the human consciousness is not so much by gradual development as by glimpses and flashes. The influx of truth comes by means of new standpoints suddenly reached, quick turns made, and grand summits gained, which open up glorious and unexpected vistas. Step by step we make a long and toilsome ascent up a steep mountain-pass, and when at length the summit is gained, as if by enchantment our eyes behold a vast expanse of sea or landscape, which before was all unrevealed. How quickly the weariness of the ascent fades out amidst the glory of the final achievement! When the morning sun gradually approaches the horizon, the forms, colors, and relations of things are disclosed by imperceptible degrees; but the intuitive perception of truth, through our deeper nature, comes more like lightning in the midst of murky darkness. New relations and realities are photographed upon our spiritual consciousness so sharply that their impress is lasting.

"Just as we leave our mortal moorings
    On the upward path,
Just so do we receive inpourings
    Of immortal faith."

The law of revelation presupposes gradual preparatory development, after which spiritual transitions are made in bounds. The experiences of Paul and Luther are good examples of the intensity of spiritual illumination when the conditions have become ripened. We do not grow into a consciousness of the divine communication, but we awaken to the Presence already within.

Divine truth is ever seeking to reveal and express itself. Upon this point Dr. Phillips Brooks, in one of his *Yale lectures*, says, "Oh, the souls which have been made sceptical by the mere clamoring of new truth to add itself to that which they have been taught to think finished and final." Truth is eternal; therefore any change in our relations with it must take place in our own consciousness. Its positive presence awaits our receptivity. If the soul be exposed to celestial rays, they will photograph their beautiful and divine features upon the sensitive higher nature. If we intently look up, in order to catch a glimpse of Truth's harmonious outlines, they will stand out in high relief to our wistful gaze.

As God is waiting to reveal Himself to man, there is no bar to reconciliation and unison but man's unreadiness. Humanity is unqualified for such Deific intimacy because of ignorance and blindness. The sun is not limited nor partial with his rays; and so God is waiting to fill every vacancy in the soul which we will make for Him. He will not force Himself into the human consciousness, but wait to be made welcome, because man's spiritual freedom is sacred. A coerced development would not be growth, for all growth must be voluntary and from within.

The fundamental law of trinity or tri-unity is seen in the zones of man's nature. He has three worlds at his disposal, even in the present material form of existence. Though all are related, their distinct boundary lines run through the nature of every human being. The higher domain we denominate the spiritual, the next the intellectual, and the third and lower, the animal or material. The spiritual world has solid proportions, here and now. When mistakenly located in the life to come, the human ego is content, for the present, to make its abode in the lower realms of its nature. Thus the normal order is inverted, and by constant habitation in the basement of its being, it clothes that part with a delusive and abnormal realism. Man's animal nature is of the earth earthy; and when his consciousness constantly dwells face to face with materiality, it takes on the quality of its sensuous environment. The sensualist dwells in a self-made world of his own color, because to him everything has a sensual hue. The human ego must turn away from sentient materialism and fit up its domicile in the nobler apartments of its nature, else it will gather its inspiration from the delusive realism of the lower plane, and come into correspondence with surrounding sliminess and debasement. Even in the intellectual realm, he who rarely, or never, mounts into the grander domain above, is "cabin'd, cribb'd, confin'd." Education, as generally defined, accompanied with all the present broad scale of material comforts and luxuries, when unassociated with spiritual development, only adds intensity to human unrest and abnormity.

God makes His dwelling-place in the higher zone of man's complex nature, and the human ego may there cultivate divine intimacy. This is the common meeting-ground between the Father and His children, face to face. Here is the serene refuge from the tempests which continually surge over the murky depths below. As man rapidly grows into correspondence with his mental environment, a homelike abode in the supreme zone of his being transmutes him into God-likeness and thus brings into manifestation the divine human type.

Formulated theology with all its accompaniments, including a literalized Bible and an authoritative sectarian standard of belief, has largely concealed the divine audience-chamber which exists in every "image of God." Current theology has put the Father far away, and usurped the place and authority of the Spirit, which is the agency that is able to "lead you into all truth." A myriad of scriptural texts which plainly teach the positive indwelling of the Spirit, are practically ignored in scholastic systems which have their foundation in external and strained interpretations, not in harmony with the great truth of the Divine Presence in the soul of man. Dogmatic teaching has made it appear that the Spirit was a gracious influence sent occasionally from a distant God, in answer to earnest importunity, but has failed to recognize its ever-present companionship, and also that it is a "Teacher." Is not such a non-recognition "the sin against the Holy Ghost"? "That He may abide with you forever," are the words used by Jesus, but such a basal principle finds scanty recognition in conventional systems.

God is Spirit; and God is everywhere. "If I ascend up into heaven, thou art there; if I make my bed in hell, behold thou art there; if I take the wings of the morning and dwell in the uttermost parts of the sea, even there shall thy hand lead me, and thy right hand shall hold me." How shall we know that we are taught and led by the Divine Mind? The evidence will be conclusive whenever we surrender the mind of self, and trustfully turn to the Infinite Will for guidance. In his letter to the Ephesians, Paul told them that they had the Holy Spirit, and therefore did not need any human teacher. Has the Church lost confidence in the ability of God to lead humanity, so that it must put up fences and bars to turn men into prescribed paths of its own?

All truth is divine. The Spirit leads men not only into religious and sacred truth, but into "all truth." Because all truth is divine, it is mighty. Overcoming all obstacles, it is constantly pressing its way toward the front for manifestation.

Its self-attesting quality fortifies it with positive evidence. It is seen to be so inseparable from God, that it clothes itself with Deific authority. Pure truth is but a synonyme for the Divine Mind. From the standpoint of the Real it is all there is.

If one calls our attention to a new material invention, theory in physics, form of government, or proposed legislation, we bring our intellectual forces to test it; but when there comes a new influx of love, faith, or spiritual aspiration from the Infinite Mind, it is sealed with the divine signet. Our deeper intuition sees at a glance the transcendent perfection of eternal principles, and feels no uncertainty regarding their acceptance. When spiritual truth flashes its pure and gentle light into the chambers of the soul, there is no mistaking its quality. Its features and vestments sparkle with original and eternal transparency.

When that which assumes to be truth is received at second-hand, cast into the fixed forms of human language, it lacks that original lustre and self-attesting quality with which it shines when poured fresh from the Father's heart into the affectionate souls of his children. From whatever outward source it may come, in the last analysis before its assimilation, it must receive the approval of the divine tribunal which is set up in the recesses of the immaterial man.

It does not follow that one is unstable in his principles, or that he yields to every new "wind of doctrine," because he keeps himself plastic to the Spirit-breathings, and responsive to its gentle leading. That which comes from within is sanctified by the divine indorsement, while from without is heard an uncertain and discordant chorus of voices.

Turning to the Fatherly communion; what inspiring influences! what delightful glimpses and surprises! what a current of paternal love! what fresh breezes! what a health-giving balm, and what a "well of pure water springing up into everlasting life"!

"Yet high above the limits of my seeing,

And folded far within the inmost heart,
And deep below the deeps of conscious being,
Thy splendor shineth: there, O God! thou art."

Truth is not a code of moral legislation, handed down to us on tablets and parchments, nor is it a formulated consensus of ecclesiastical wisdom; but it is a disclosing of God's features and methods within the human consciousness.

He is a dull learner who believes that Divine revealment is in any manner limited to the Bible, or that the writers of the Sacred Word received divine truth in any different manner, or through any more exclusive channel, than other devout and transparent souls. They were mountain-peaks among a wilderness of foothills. In degree they were pre-eminent, but their indwelling wisdom came from the same primal Source from which all other receptive ones gather their inspiration. The theory that the Bible is "the only divine rule of faith and practice," as dogmatically set forth in creeds and confessions, is not only dishonoring to the ever-present "Teacher," but is out of accord with the Scriptures themselves. They nowhere make such an unfounded claim, which, in itself, must be accounted a grave abuse of their beautiful and sacred office. Things may be revealed to babes which remain hid to trained intellects, who measure all truth by textual statement or legal definition.

Systematic theology has missed much of the divine overflowing in the soul of man, because of its rigid mechanical theories, which practically bury all revelation in the Bible, taking it for granted that the scriptural channel is the only one. Thus the Book has been seriously misinterpreted by its zealous but injudicious defenders. It lays no claim to a self-limited inspiration, but proclaims its office as the Word which quickeneth; as the great auxiliary influence to guide the world to direct inspiration. It points out the road to divine munificence, but makes no claim to a monopoly of its possession. It leads to the living Christ, who is the unfolding revealment of the Father, and in whom are hid treasures of Wisdom and Knowledge.

There is much concern at present in some branches of the Church because of heresy, which is defined as being a divergence from formulated confessions; but the great and real heresy of the present age is the non-recognition of the "Comforter." Such an offence is directly against the indwelling Spirit. The rejection of the Holy Spirit makes forgiveness impossible while such an attitude continues, because the question is one of condition, and not of punishment from without. Forgiveness is not a remission of penalty, but a change of character; a substitution of the Christ Mind for the mind of the flesh. Real forgiveness has none of the aspects of a debit and credit transaction, and does not merely signify an escape from natural consequences. By the vital operation of a new life, which we call regeneration, salvation—which is forgiveness—comes as an invariable result. The overcoming power of the divine influx frees from the power of sin, and the resultant forgiveness consists in that very fact, so there is nothing supernatural in the process.

The Spirit never goes or comes except to human consciousness. "He shall abide with you forever:" but without our co-operation there is no fruitful vitality. Unrecognized, there is a sense in which He is absent. Christ told His disciples that He must go away, in order that the Comforter might come. The Incarnation so covered the field of their sensuous vision, that they were unable to behold the greater spiritual Presence while the outward embodiment remained before them. The Christ Himself recognized this tendency as a real limitation belonging to His material expression, and His plain statement of this fact is deeply significant. "It is expedient for you that I go away." The Incarnate saw the strong inclination of the human mind to fasten itself to material forms, instead of looking beyond such expressions, and grasping the grander unexpressed Presence. The eyes of the world have been focused upon the historic Jesus, rather than upon the indwelling immaterial Christ who is God (Spirit) with us. While Jesus was present His disciples gained no spiritual self-reliance: they forsook Him in the hour of danger; they often failed in their attempts at healing; and they depended upon kingly and material power, because their eyes were holden to the essential Saviour. Even the naturally brave and impetuous Peter denied his present Lord; and when ecclesiastical bitterness ripened into persecution and arrest, His disciples deserted him in the most cowardly manner. After the Resurrection they rapidly caught the spiritual import of His mission. When bodily limitations were removed they became boldly conscious of the unlimited spiritual Presence. They who had been weak, cowardly, vacillating, became teachers, leaders, and heroes. No disease was too deadly for them to heal; no danger too great for them to face; no persecution daunted them; and no obstacle was insurmountable. Paul, in referring to past material limitations, expressed this vital principle: "Therefore henceforth know we no man after the flesh: yea, though we have known Christ after the flesh, yet now henceforth know we Him no more." The world and the theologies are still strongly inclined to know Christ after the flesh. The cross and the death receive that emphasis which belongs to the imparted life. Jesus was not the Christ, except as He was His embodiment. It is the living Christ of to-day which the world needs, rather than His material expression of eighteen centuries ago. This great substitution in the world-consciousness has been a sad mistake; and it presents the most notable example of resting in the letter and form, and missing the Spirit and Reality. The great Spiritual Vision is intended for all races and generations as much as for the immediate disciples. "These works shall follow them that believe," and them that believe are not limited by time nor condition. Healing was one of the "works," but it has not "followed" since the times of the primitive Church. The "greater things than I have done" which Christ promised, have been signally lacking in their realization. There can be no valid reason given why all the "works" ought not to abound in the church of to-day. The decadence of spirituality, and the materialism and scholasticism which made religion more of a system than an inner life, account for the loss of the healing power. When worldliness and ecclesiastical pomp and authority crept into the church, her practical vitality faded out.

Spiritual harmony should find outward demonstration and expression in physical and mental wholeness. "Ye therefore shall be perfect as your heavenly Father is perfect." (Revised version.) The "fall" from a spiritual to a ruling material consciousness imposes upon us the limitations and disorders of the unspiritual realm. In proportion as we yield controlling allegiance to the material body and its environment, we build our own prison walls and pass into a condition of servitude.

There is One Spirit, but it has a variety of manifestations. The world is gradually making the discovery that pure and unselfish love is the essence of vital religion. It has taken almost nineteen hundred years for it to find out the depth of Jesus' declaration, that the whole law is fulfilled in Love; and the lesson is not yet fully learned.

The day of Pentecost was a period of wonderful divine revelations, not because of any unusual willingness on the God-ward side, but on account of a greatly ripened receptivity. The disciples had thought deeply upon the spiritual meaning of Christ's mission since the human embodiment was withdrawn; and with many predictions fresh in mind, they were in a condition of intense expectancy. The oneness of their burning desire brought them together without any plan or appointment. They were inspired with that joyous harmony which binds Divinity and Humanity together, and with "one accord" they gave expression, in various forms, to the spiritual illumination which filled them to overflowing. They were aflame with the "Consuming Fire" of Love, and this bound them more closely together than the ties of any outward organization could have done. It was a day of first fruits; the earliest ripening of that great spiritual harvest which is being gathered among all the nations. There is no hint of any constitution, confession, or ritual, but there was a grand kindling and influx of new life. The quickened vitality was so unselfish in its manifestations, that they, without any feeling of sacrifice, and as a matter of privilege, give up their life-long accumulations for the common weal. There was no forced communism, nor legislative socialism from without, but a repletion of love, without any element of self or self-seeking. The scene presented a localized millennium; a prophetic object-lesson of that time "when all shall know the Lord"—or be conscious of His presence in them, "from the least even unto the greatest."

"Then, go not thou in search of Him,
But to thyself repair;
Wait thou within the silence dim,
And thou shalt find Him there."

But a small part of the historical evidence of the truth of the gospel is in dusty tomes or ancient parchments; but it is contained in the human experience of divine companionship. There is no other proof comparable to demonstration.

The spiritual world is often inseparably connected with the future state, and that is the main reason why so many regard it as incomprehensible. Rather, it is here and now a world of reality and substance. It is the material world which is the realm of shadows and unreality. If our faculties are attuned, it is our privilege to live in the spiritual world under present conditions,—to enjoy its fellowships, learn its lessons, and bask in its sunshine. The inward ministry of the Spirit is the vital nourishment which feeds to its full fruition the whole complex human nature. Inspiration is a force, a divine motive-power behind human expressiveness; and it imparts its quality without in the least encroaching upon man's freedom and spontaneity. The sensuous personality contends against the abiding divine Presence, and persistently claims an independent selfhood of its own. It would displace the true ego of the divine image, and install its false and material self. What slime of animalism and selfish materialism clings to us unless we earnestly draw a sharp line of demarcation, and absolutely deny the power of all that is below it!

Conventional theology has practically made the Holy Spirit a rare and unfamiliar visitor. Can we have the divine companionship upon easy terms and under every-day circumstances? Yea, verily, if we expect and welcome it. We must feel it as a present Companion and Guest. When the noise of the outer world is hushed, and its cares and ambitions barred out, if we listen we may hear the "still, small voice."

"From God derived, to God by nature joined,
  We act the dictates of His mighty mind;
  Though priests are mute and temples still,
  God never wants a voice to speak His will."

If we earnestly invite spiritual illumination, it will come in and flood the soul-chambers with its golden light as surely as air inclines to a vacuum. We can link ourselves to the living Christ: He in us and we in Him, and such a tie is most natural. The unfolding of the Presence within touches our threefold being in its entire breadth. If friends desert, "there is One who sticketh closer than a brother." There can be no loneliness; it is only a seeming. He is our completeness; for apart from Him there is a radical deficiency. St. Paul says, "Ye are complete in Him." What a glorious assurance! Not shall be, but *are*. Have we discovered it? MacDonald beautifully expresses such a sentiment: "He who has the Spirit of God, God Himself in him, has the Life in him, possesses the final cure of all ill, and has in himself the answer to all possible prayer." To be in Him, He must be enthroned in our consciousness. When physically or mentally disordered we are not "complete." But we turn to outward and material things for help, instead of looking inward to the Great Restorer. When we might have emancipation, we prefer to wear the galling yoke of material servitude. "The last must be first," and the material become immaterial. So long as the pleasures and pains of our lower or physical organism occupy the "chief seats" in our consciousness, we are captives, even if the clanking of our chains be unheard.

For man,—made as he is in "the image of God,"—spiritual rule is normal, logical, and scientific. The reverse condition is inverted and abnormal, and its penalties inherent.

"The secret place of the Most High" is not a poetic fiction, but a veritable retreat where the Divine and the Human meet in loving embrace. The haze of theological complication is passing away, and we need no longer confine our search for the Father to ordinances and sacraments. "The Kingdom of Heaven is within you." Material wealth is not to be had for the asking, but immaterial treasures are waiting for room to bestow themselves.

"God is Spirit," and His revealment to man must be made through the medium of Spirit. If He were possessed of a material form, the way of recognition would be through the sensuous faculties. Spirit can only be spiritually discerned. God cannot be seen in the Bible, nor in Nature, except through the exercise of the spiritual vision. There may be various approaches, but there is but one highway of communication, and that is where God and man touch and become one, and thus bridge the chasm. Man can aspire to nothing more lofty than a distinct and ruling God-consciousness.

The modern Church in its anxiety to be practical has become external. The Occidental races and religions, though holding Oriental forms of thought in light esteem, have much to learn from them regarding the paramount importance of spiritual introspection. Christ taught that it was the sinful thought which constituted the offence as much as the act which gave it expression. The recognized presence of God is the antidote for sin and sinful thinking. They cannot abide the divine fellowship.

"The Kingdom of God cometh not with observation." The disciples looked for outward signs, and likewise the modern world judges by external appearances. The supreme forces of the Universe are unseen. Multitudes are unconsciously led by the Spirit, who do not realize that its gentle guidance is deeper than their conscious personality. The strings of their spiritual nature vibrate responsively to the breath of God, bringing out tones which have unearthly sweetness, even though their harmony cannot be fully realized without human co-operation. If we would reap the golden harvest of Spirit, we must sow and cultivate in accordance with its laws. Conforming to divine methods. Infinite Power is enlisted in our service, but disregarding them, we "fight against God."

The world is moving steadily up to a condition when the spiritual or real man will overcome and hold under control that seeming man, the sensuous counterpart. There is a desperate struggle going on between the lower and higher types, in which the former are being vanquished, for all life is being lifted toward God. The whole creation is groaning and travailing, and the day of complete emancipation will at length be ushered in with great rejoicing. The signs of a more general spiritual interpretation of God, Nature, and the Bible, are multiplying on every hand. The spirit of unity is disintegrating sectarian barriers. The great altruistic current is gaining volume, and Love is broadening its channels, and growing more divine and impersonal. We are under the "Dispensation of the spirit," and modern progress and upliftment indicate the more general recognition of the fact, that all laws and all truth are divine. The time comes on apace "when all shall know the Lord," not merely in a restricted theological sense, but as the Omnipresent Inspirer of Humanity.

IV. Biblical Revelation.

THE BIBLE is a vast storehouse. It contains treasures of priceless value, unlimited variety, and general adaptability. Its supplies are suited to the requirements of every age, race, and condition. Its doors are always open; its riches to be had for the asking; and, unlike material depositories, demands upon it do not diminish its resources. The Biblical framework, with its various partitions, shelves, and cases, has only a nominal value; but within it are contained royal treasures and gifts,—"gold, frankincense, and myrrh."

The Written Word is also like a great mine. There are shafts, tunnels, and galleries; engines, wheels, and pulleys; there is pumping, draining, hoisting, and assorting; and afterwards, stamping, melting, and moulding. What is the purpose of all this activity? and have all these complex processes any special significance? Is there order and unity in the midst of such seeming confusion? The bars of bright and shining metal, which are the final result of these energetic operations, furnish the answer. The treasure was hid, and could only be extracted, reduced, and purified by such a severe and searching process. There are deep veins of truth imbedded in the strata of national history; and rich specimens of the ore of virtue, wisdom, love, and self-sacrifice, cropping out above the surface of individual character in patriarchs, kings, peasants, and slaves. The pure gold and silver of the Spirit are found in an endless variety of combinations and degrees of richness. Some of its ores are free and easily separated, and others are refractory and difficult of reduction to the pure metal of truth. There must be much crushing and heating before the golden product can be released from the grasp of its local combinations. If the whole mining territory were solid gold, the metal would lose its rarity and extreme value. An important element of its great worth consists in the labor and patience involved in its production. The unprecedented study and searching criticism of the Bible which characterize the present era are but a more vigorous working of the mine, not for its destruction nor its exhaustion, but in order to the production of greater wealth.

The Bible is a library rather than a book; but notwithstanding its marvellous variety, it does not claim to be a complete or finished revelation. But if it does not contain all truth, its pages glow with spiritual pictures which have every variety of coloring, foreground, and perspective. It is richly garnished with jewels; but their polish, setting, and framing, show wide diversity. But though it is precious, it is not a fetich which possesses any miraculous charm, nor a divinity to be worshipped, but rather a great consensus of experiences and object-lessons. It furnishes compass, chart, and steering directions for the voyage of life. It is not an end, but an important means to an end. Truth does not originate in its pages, nor gain its authority from textual declarations, because it eternally existed. Truth is not true because the Bible says so; but the Bible says so because it was already, and is everlastingly, true. The sole use of the collective Inspired Library—voluminous though it may be—is to teach men two very brief rules of action, or rather principles of living,—love to God and love to man. These are the concentrated golden product of the wonderful profusion of law, history, psalmody, prophecy, and philosophy, which make up the Old and New Testaments. The human mind is so constituted that it does not readily assimilate concentrated, abstract truth; otherwise, the great collection of Sacred Writings might at once be reduced to a simple statement of the two all-inclusive motives before noted. That this fine gold of principle may be received and transmuted into living spiritual fibre, it must be presented in all possible combinations and conditions; seen at all angles and in different lights, and tested in its application to varying ages, nations, and civilizations. Its essence must flow into the lives of rich and poor, high and low; its quality must be exhibited in all stages of development, from germ-planting through successive stages of growth, to blossoming and full fruition; its energy must be brought into contact with prosperity and adversity, knowledge and ignorance, nations and individuals.

The Bible is like a great mirror for every class and condition. Though in itself a grand Unit, each one sees it from a different side, and catches an aspect not quite like that of any other. It has one message, but many interpretations; one melody, but endless variations. Objectively it is always the same, but the diverse color of the lenses through which it is viewed gives it all possible hues. Unchangeable in itself, it is always changing in significance, even to the same individual in different moods and periods. To each observer—in the last analysis—it is not the real objective Bible which is the Bible *to him*, but it is his conception of it that is the veritable Book. From diverse subjective colorings, scores of sects and denominations find their peculiar creeds and theologies in the One Book. The Calvinist and Methodist, the Quaker and the Baptist, the Trinitarian and the Unitarian, all find an abundance of what they look for. It is "all things to all men," because, as in a mirror, all see their own reflection. If every word and punctuation point were of divine dictation, so that the Scripture writers were amanuenses, pure and simple, and we had a perfect translation of their messages, the diversity of doctrinal interpretation would not thereby be diminished.

The nature of scriptural inspiration is one of the burning problems of this closing decade of the nineteenth century, for we are passing through a period of wonderful transition. The Bible has been burdened with a heavy load of literalism, superstition, and fetichism, which is now being swept away by what is known as the "Higher Criticism," and by a rational interpretation of that which constitutes inspiration. The demand that God-given reason should be held in abeyance when the Book was approached, has given it an unnatural and mechanical character. The Roman church withheld it from the masses lest they might misinterpret it, and ecclesiastical Protestantism has put supernatural restrictions upon it for much the same reason. There has been a feeling that the Book could not be trusted to stand alone,—upon its merits,—and that some kind of priestly explanation must accompany it. As if its inherent spiritual quality and power were not sufficiently plain to show its divine character, the theologies have been impelled to "steady the Ark of the Lord" by supernatural and superstitious props and defences. The Bible is abundantly able to take care of itself. The evidence of its being an embodiment of divine truth is inherent, rather than from without. It is not dependent upon the authenticity of its reputed writers; the historic genuineness of its ancient manuscripts; nor even upon the accuracy of its translations,—desirable as these all may be,—but in its lifelike portrayal of human character and its needs, and in its power to energize life and motive. The real test of all inspiration lies in the measure of its ability to inspire.

The theory of verbal inspiration, including literal inerrancy, which so many sincere but unwise Biblicists think it necessary to maintain as a "defence" of the Book, renders it inharmonious, eliminates its human element, and mars its practical adaptability. Carried to its logical conclusion it would make the Infinite to be the Author of self-evident imperfection. But such a logical result is hardly followed out, because, at a blow, it would obliterate all the individual freedom and personality of the writers, the evidence of which shines out in every chapter. But those who feel it to be a necessity to defend verbal inspiration, do not choose to consider the necessary result, but leave the subject at some indefinable point midway. The transition from the literalism of past periods, to a deeper and more spiritual interpretation, is general and rapid. Many deplore it with undoubted sincerity or undisguised alarm, and believe it to be progress toward less or no religion; but it is safe to assume that nothing intrinsic will be lost. If external and arbitrary Biblical authority be in some degree weakened, the manifold strengthening from within will render abundant compensation.

Verbal inspiration has been held as a protective doctrine, but its power to promote moral or spiritual energy is wanting. It has been relied upon more as a security and authority for doctrinal belief, than as a force to quicken life. Every sect has used it as an armor to defend its peculiar tenets, more than as an energizing motive and tonic. The prevailing conception of the nature of the Book has been rigid in form, but deficient in vitality. It has been held sacred as a source of correct theology, but its power to infuse God-consciousness is largely unrecognized. Its spiritual energy is the highest and only test of its divine truthfulness, while verbal inerrancy is a technicality, and invites attention to "the letter that killeth," rather than to the "Spirit which giveth life." The letter appeals to the intellectual faculty, but only the Spirit can infuse new life and convey spiritual momentum. Ancient history, law, and prophecy, and also the teaching of Christ and his Apostles, must be translated into fresh and personal manifestation.

The "Higher Criticism" is useful, not because of its discovery that the so-called Mosaic writings are the work of various authors, nor because in general it more correctly locates authorship and discriminates regarding the local and peculiar conditions under which books were written, nor even because it recognizes both the divine and human elements, but for the reason that it approaches the Book impartially—as it would any other book—for what it really is. It is eminently a Book of common-sense; and the removal of its ecclesiastical, doctrinal, and denominational bandages greatly increases its transforming power in daily life. It is an armory filled with spiritual weapons. It is not especially a Sunday book, nor a special message which requires peculiar and official interpretation, but an ever-available Invigorator and Restorer.

If the Scriptures were inerrant in detail, they could not be a progressive revelation, for there would be no room for progress; but because they do contain a fallible element, they are adapted to human needs. If the inspired writers received their revelations in some supernatural or abnormal manner, their experiences would have little value for us. Those men of old would thereby constitute an order by themselves, and, follow them as we might, we could never be fellow-sharers of the same powers and privileges which they enjoyed.

It is only through the intellectual faculty that there can be any possible danger of confusing the divine and human elements of the Inspired Word. Its intrinsic lessons and spiritual delineations can only be discerned and measured by the inner perception, and by such discernment they need not be mistaken. The fine gold of love, faith, truth, life, and spirituality, constitutes the true inerrancy. The imperfection of the human element of the Bible only makes the pure quality of its truth in the spiritual realm more conspicuous. Only with humanity intermingled with divinity in the Word would it be practically comprehensible. It does not try to separate God from human consciousness, but to bring Him nearer; yea, to show Him as in us, the illuminating and energizing force. The Decalogue was inscribed in man's nature long before it was graven upon tablets of stone. The world has looked upon the Bible as a code of divine legislation, a great and comprehensive "Thou shalt not;" but it is rather an emancipation proclamation. The love of God, wrought into the lives of men of old,—men like us,—through all the lights and shadows of human experience, brings out in high relief the ideals to be sought, and the mistakes to be avoided in the uneven pilgrimage over which they passed far in advance of us.

Up to the time of Luther and the Reformation, religion, theology, and authority were centred in the organized Church; but since that time, among the Protestant branches, everything has crystallized around the Book. There is a tendency ever manifesting itself in humanity to build from without rather than from within.

The general law of evolution is so distinctly written upon all animate and inanimate creation, that its general acceptance, as a process, is becoming almost universal. Though still so far, far below his ideal condition, man has progressed, instead of retrograded, though there is a sense in which his future potentiality was present when the first breath of the divine spiritual life was breathed into him. The Bible in itself is a notable example of evolutionary unfoldment. Starting on a low plane, there is a steady though slow development and refinement in the quality and standard of its delineations of human character, from Genesis to Revelation. The grand scope and purpose of the unrolled panorama of Sacred Literature, is the evolution of the ideal spiritual man from the animal selfhood. Here is evolution which is worthy of the name, because an infinite leap upward is taken, even though the latent force which makes it possible has been in a process of accumulation through the eons of the unfathomable past. God's moral economy is unchangeable and perfect, and human conceptions are slowly approaching toward it, as shown by higher standards from age to age. If the Bible were purely a divine book, the Patriarchal ideals of character would be as pure and lofty as those of John and Paul. The standard of righteousness, even among the beacon lights of Old Testament history, was low, although they towered far above their contemporaries, and, for their times, lived very near to God. It is not irreverent to suggest that their comprehension of Him may be said to have been great in quantity, but moderate in quality. To a greater or less extent they were given to polygamy, sensuality, and slavery, and even the great Psalmist of Israel, who was said to be "a man after God's own heart," was guilty of many heinous offences. The authors of Sacred Writ lived and wrote under all the limitations and weaknesses that are common to mankind, otherwise their experiences would contain no living lessons for us. Their records show a continual growth and unfoldment in the apprehension of spiritual truth, both in individual and collective life, during the broad period covered by the Inspired Narratives. Man will know more to-morrow than to-day; and no consistent interpretation of the Scriptures can be made, except in the light of this principle. In any other way the Book loses its cohesion and unity, and becomes unintelligible. The sceptic says to the literalist: "Your Bible indorses slavery and polygamy, and sanctions war and revenge;" and the literalist cannot deny this from his own method of interpretation. There is hardly a doctrine so irrational, or a course of conduct so gross, that isolated texts cannot be found, by the letter of which they are inculcated or may be defended; yet, disregarding such plain inferences, some of the leading dogmas—as, for instance, those regarding election and future endless punishment—have for their whole foundation a strained construction of less than half a dozen verses of the whole Bible. What a wonderful elevation in the standard of human conduct and spiritual consciousness took place in the period between Noah and John; yet the former, no less than the latter, towered far above the standards of the age in which he lived.

The blind acceptance of the supposed necessary theory of Biblical infallibility has been an incubus upon the Church, and has largely shorn the Book of its living power to inspire. Such an assumption has made it appear at once unreasonable, unattractive, and unnatural. The well-meaning men who imagined that they were doing "God service" by a zealous defence of his Book, unwittingly made it so contradictory and unlovable, that mankind—who so much need its lessons—have been repelled from it.

The Scriptures are not a revelation, but are records of revelations; the treasure, in varying degrees of richness, being contained "in earthen vessels." Reasonable interpretation makes them incomparably the most beautiful, harmonious, and profitable of all literature. Through them, from first to last, runs a golden chain without a missing link. The dogmaticians have buried the Bible beneath confessions and scholastic systems; and it is for these, rather than for the Book, that they are concerned. Their use of it has been secondary and defensive; as a breast-work for the protection of institutions and systems. Thousands have been kept from its earnest study because of unwarranted claims that inspiration is verbal, and that its authority depends upon the acceptance of traditional theories of authorship, and the accuracy of ancient manuscripts with their perfect translation and preservation.

"We live by faith: but faith is not the slave

Of text and legend. Reason's voice and God's,
Nature's and duty's, never are at odds."

The literalists are very determined against a "rational" study of the Word, because such a fair interpretation of its teachings will endanger their systems; but they can as easily keep back the tides of the Atlantic, as arrest the great transition, stifle the spirit of modern inquiry, or suppress the desire for unadulterated truth.

It is not within the province of this work to make any critical or detailed analysis of the Bible, nor of its history and composition. The rich and growing literature of the "Higher Criticism," and the able and comprehensive teaching of eminent pioneers in the work of Biblical disenthralment, like Professors Briggs, Harper, Dr. Abbott, and many others, furnishes abundant evidence of the harmony between a reasonable theory of inspiration and scholarly and exhaustive technical research.

As the Sacred Literature of the Jews makes up the canon of the Scriptures, the world is indebted to the Hebrew race for its Christian Bible. It is a Semitic Book; and yet, as the Jewish race is a factor of the great human family, its remarkable experiences and their lessons have a universal adaptability. The fact, however, that it was written by men of the East, and is thoroughly Oriental in tone and coloring, must not be over-looked. Its warm, picturesque allegory, parable, poetry, and hyperbole, are with difficulty transmuted, unimpaired, into cold English phraseology. Eternal principles never change, but their accessories may be of infinite variety. The earnest seeker after truth need not be baffled, for true spiritual discernment plunges far beneath the changeable surface of race, time, and custom. Just here is an abundance of "inerrancy." Unselfish love, faith, truth, and spirituality, are entities which have the same divine sparkle and fixity in all possible combinations.

Other races and peoples besides the Hebrews have their records of revelations which contain divine elements; but "the Bible is incomparably superior to them in quality and power. It is a graphic and earnest history of individuals, families, tribes, and races, in the process of spiritual evolution. Its production was in every respect natural, and involved no suspension of divine laws nor supernatural interposition. As its writers were moved by the Holy Ghost, so other writers and other men, then and now, are inspired in like manner when under similar spiritual condition and development. Any other theory presupposes a changeable and partial Deity, rather than He "who is without variableness or shadow of turning."

The inspired Book is like a vast landscape, rich and varied, both in foreground and perspective. There are majestic mountain peaks whose summits pierce the clouds; peaceful valleys containing green pastures; trees and plants, waving grain and blooming flowers, fruitful gardens and sandy wastes, purling brooks and mighty rivers, lowing herds and gentle flocks, rocks, pitfalls, precipices, fog, sunshine, and shadow. Law, History, Poetry, and Prophecy, in the Old Testament, and the higher ethical and more spiritual teaching in the Gospels and Epistles of the New, are mingled in changing proportions in the different periods of the unique history of the Hebrew nation. Upon the surface of this great swift-flowing current are seen the simple dignity of patriarchal and pastoral life, the cruelty of slavery, institutes of priestly orders and sacrificial offerings, the government of judgeship, the authority of kingship, graceful poetry, and metrical psalmody, weary ages of captivity, prophetic teaching and warning. Messianic expectancy, fulfilment, tragedy, spiritual baptism, persecution, the planting of churches, and racial dispersion.

What wonderful life-lessons are dramatically portrayed in the grand epic poem of Job; and its impressiveness does not depend upon its historic verity, any more than does the significance of the "Parable of the Ten Virgins." The Psalms of David, which are full of pictures of ever-changing and diverse spiritual moods, are equally instructive and true to nature, whether written by the royal Psalmist or by a score of less-known authors. The letters to the "Seven Churches" would have the same applicability if addressed to the churches of the world, as they had to those of a little corner of western Asia.

The Sacred Hebrew Writings make up a grand chorus of warning, reproof, discipline, incentive, and inspiration.

"Over and over again,
No matter which way we turn,
We always find in the Book of Life
Some lessons we have to learn."

The Inspired Book touches every life in its full breadth, and at every point. That supreme spiritual aspiration and God-consciousness that illumined men of old will inspire men of today. Those great divine sources and springs have not lost their power to kindle new life. The history of the Jewish nation is a grand drama, the ever-shifting scenes of which portray vice and virtue worked out in character and life, each to their legitimate result. With natural, free interpretation of the Book, its light will grow clearer and broader, and it will be an ever unfolding source of inspiration to human life.

V. Revelation Through the Son.

O DIVINE human mystery! Can Infinity be contained in finite form? O supreme wonder! old, yet ever new. Thou art wrapped in our mantle, and we see Thee as one of us. We look into Thine eyes, and feel the loving presence of an Elder Brother. As we fondly gaze upon Thy divine lineaments our own hard features are transformed into Thy likeness. Our vision is clarified and our courage quickened. We turn confidingly to Thee, and are not abashed at Thy glory. The overflowing of Thy love arouses a kindred response and awakens new life in us.

When the world was shrouded in darkness a Star arose. Its dazzling light revealed the deep hidden lines of Divinity in humanity. Old and young were entranced by its beauty. Wise men from afar hastened to yield their homage, and shepherds hailed the Prince of peace. The radiance of the Star lighted the faces of all who turned towards it, and its warm glow dried their tears. Its beams penetrated into souls, illumined their dark recesses, and quickened in them the germs of their divine nature. Its light made a bright pathway before those who had lost their way in dark mazes and bogs. Its rays transformed the briers which lined the pathway of weary feet into roses which filled the air with their fragrance. Under its genial influence the hardness of life's duties and pursuits softened. It shone into prison-houses, and the chains of captives melted away, and they went free. The illumination left no dark hiding-places where gloom and pain could find a lodgement. The air vibrated with song, and was redolent with the fragrance of heaven.

"The dayspring from on high shall visit us,
To shine upon them that sit in darkness and the shadow of death;
To guide our feet into the way of peace."

The morning dawned after a long, long, wearisome night, and the great undercurrent of earnest expectation found fulfilment. Who is this that gathers both the divine and human life-currents, and is known as the Son of God and Son of man? Jesus was the eternal Christ in outward expression. "God is Spirit; and therefore the Son of God was, and is. Spirit, as are also all sons of God. Paul, in one of his letters to the Corinthians, says, "But we have the mind of Christ." This was true, but only Jesus had it in perfect fulness.

The demonstration of God's character is the supreme lesson needed by the human race. To know God is eternal life, and the impartation of that knowledge opens the way of salvation. There has always existed in the depths of man's nature an intense yearning for some medium through which God could be comprehended. There have been "saviours" who have risen up among all nations, and in all ages. Moses, Joshua, Elijah, Isaiah, and Ezekiel were among the long list of demonstrators of God in different periods of Jewish history, but none of them fulfilled the expectation of a supreme Mediator who would be the Messiah. The anticipation was general, but yet the prevailing ideal of Israel was a low one. The "Anointed" was to be a powerful king, who would deliver his chosen people from their enemies, and restore their national glory and prestige. He would establish a magnificent temporal kingdom. Only a few who were upon the "watchtowers of Zion" caught any glimpses of the light of that broader spiritual kingdom of whose dominion there shall be no end. The true nature of the Christian economy could hardly be discerned, except by those lesser saviours whose eyes were open to the heavenly ideal. They alone were able to look from the mountain-tops of spiritual attainment and catch the sublime significance of God manifested in the flesh. But with all the popular misapprehension, the expected advent was the loftiest theme of law, poetry, and prophecy. The light of the Christian dispensation in the hearts and consciences of men shone backward as well as forward. Its anticipation kindled and quickened spiritual aspiration. The patient waiting at length blossomed into glorious realization, and this forms the great theme of Evangelistic and Apostolic inspiration.

The interchangeable use of the terms Jesus and Christ, and their seeming identity in theological statements, has caused much misapprehension. Christ signifies the eternal outflow of God's love toward man, as we view it on the man-ward side. This Love is one with God, and is God; but to our vision it has the aspect of a separate personality. God being absolute and unknowable to material sense, it follows that men of undeveloped spirituality must have some material expression to enable them to get glimpses of the divine character. We speak of love and faith as abstract entities, and yet the human mind can hardly grasp them except through forms of personal manifestation. God's love flows out toward His children as naturally as light and heat are radiated from the sun. He fills the universe, and He is Love; and Love is therefore the one all-inclusive principle. Christ is the name, not of the material Jesus, but of the principle or spirit that expressed itself through His organism. Jesus is called "the Christ;" the latter term signifying his office or quality. Jesus was the name of a Judean peasant, whose conditions were material, local, and temporal, while Christ is from everlasting to everlasting. Prevailing materialism, now as in the times of Jesus, is ever dwelling upon forms and expressions. The key to the mystery of the Incarnation is found in the comprehension of the fact, that perfect, ideal manhood signifies complete oneness with God. The intrinsic man (God's image) is spirit, and his physical organism forms no part of him. Its use is for expression on the present plane. But man has built up a false personality out of his material consciousness, so that his absolute or divine selfhood is obscured and often unrecognized.

It is unprofitable to dogmatize about the Incarnation, but we may try to interpret it by its own light. The attempt of scholastics to technically analyze the nature of God and man united ends in an unfathomable sea of speculation. Intellectually the most earnest and honest observers see it on opposite sides. Some look upon Jesus as "very God," and others as very man, and still others as one distinct person of the three who comprise the Trinity. Some believe that, in consequence of a great emergency, "a plan" was formed in the deep councils of the Godhead for the redemption of the world, and that Christ volunteered to undertake the mission. He came from a far-away heaven, and by substitution put his righteousness in the place of man's sinfulness, thus vindicating the divine justice and satisfying the claims of broken law. The threefold aspect of God thus becomes Christian polytheism. How dogmatic, hard, and mechanical!

What is more natural and reasonable than that the substance of the divine Father should be incarnated? Nearly all religions have held that in some way God, or the gods, have assumed material embodiment as a means of lifting up humanity. The imperfect incarnations of the ancient heathen nations were but the out-croppings of this universal soul-craving. We long for Fatherly sympathy and communion. The tendrils of our common nature reach out toward God to feel after and know Him, and such a demand is a natural prophecy of supply. The beauty and perfection of the divine economy are found in the harmonious adjustment of supply and demand. Infinite wisdom has fitted these elements for each other in perfect proportion, whether in the spiritual, intellectual, or physical realm. May we not regard the embodiment of the Christ-mind in Jesus as the divine creative response to that very craving which He has implanted in the soul of man?

How can the limitless omnipresent Deity manifest Himself through such a puny channel as the human organism? Infinity cannot be diminished, but is not a drop of ocean spray one with its parent source? An unworthy similitude, for spirit is measureless and incomparable.

A quickened spiritual nature may know God directly through its own consciousness, but unregenerate and material selfhood must have a message in its own language. God's substance must be cast into human form, else sensuous understanding cannot encompass it; therefore the "Word was made flesh." Other sages and saviours have taught the loftiest morality, but none have perfectly embodied it. They gave intellectual expression to truth, but Christ was Truth itself. Jesus the Christ was "the Way, the Truth, and the Life," perfectly filling the divine type. The branches of the human vine are loaded with clusters which are shrunken and acrid, but here was sweet and perfected fruit. In slow, wearisome stages we are pressing on toward that ideal which in Him was actualized. He was perfected through suffering, and made manifest that law of self-abnegation, through the experience of which men must pass before they can become "sons of God."

But we must not forget that Christ, though living in the material Jesus, really dwelt in the kingdom of spirit. The outer shell of humanity softened that light, in order that its brilliancy might not be too dazzling. Though of perfected type, he was yet man, and understood the meaning of human imperfection, and experienced its trials and temptations. With a perfect command of divine law, and a mental environment of ideal roundness and purity, he was able to project such conditions into the minds of others, and thus perform wonderful works. Right in the midst of this restless, sensuous world there is existent an unseen but veritable kingdom of spiritual harmony. In this ideal domain he lived, and the purpose of his incarnate life was to introduce his followers into its delectable realities. Its beautiful conditions are possible while we dwell in the present state. "Behold the kingdom of Heaven is within you." Christ came to establish a rule of spirit, in comparison with which earthly thrones and dynasties are barren forms of organized selfishness. "He that loseth his life shall save it." What an enigma such a declaration has been to a world that judges from outside appearances! "God manifest in the flesh"—presents the perfect human pattern. With archetypal purity placed before us, material attainment is found to be hollow and unsatisfying.

The Incarnation was not necessary to show that God could take the form of man, but that man can become like God. The divine quality of the Christ-life cannot be believed unless it be felt.

"Ah, would thy heart but be a manger for the birth,
  God would once more become a child on earth."

The fulness of the Father in the Son is a sublime truth that is above dependence upon historic or miraculous evidence, because the vital force of the "mind of Christ" in man is self-attesting. It is not a mere re-enforcement along lines already occupied, but a turning, a changed direction, regeneration.

The vital fact of the Christly embodiment is not affected by the non-acceptance of any particular theory of the manner in which it took place. Even were it to be conceded that Joseph was the natural father of Jesus, it does not in the least affect the spiritual truth of the Incarnation, and the same free solution is as applicable to the material resurrection. If the Spirit of God, in its fulness, seeks human embodiment for our spiritual enlightenment, why should it not incarnate itself in accordance with existing order? Without dogmatizing upon this point, how can it be unreasonable to think that it was wholly human, for otherwise it would hardly be upon our plane. Of the material resurrection, the author of a recent able work, "A Washington Bible Class," says, "If in some tomb, hewn out of solid rock, there should be discovered to-day the unquestionable body of our Lord, wound in the linen clothes, with the hundred-pound weight of myrrh and aloes wherewith loving friends had laid it to rest—none the less, Christ the Lord is risen to-day. Nothing can be more narrow than to limit the ways, the modes, by which God shall enter His World, by which spirit-force shall impress itself upon matter, by which the ever-immanent shall reveal itself to the finite.

We are to study the incarnation as we find it in the unbroken sequences of nature, in the long history of man, through that infallible revelation which God constantly makes of himself in his works of creation, providence, and redemption."

The vital truth of the Incarnation is a thousandfold more important than the method of its outward details. The unsoundness of other than traditional views upon these doctrines has been recently affirmed by an ecclesiastical court,[2] and the event has caused much discussion, as to the proper boundaries for liberty of opinion. Christianity is grievously wounded in the house of its friends when its essential life is bound up with any particular aspect of non-essential circumstances. The cause of pure religion has received untold injury from the assumption that its superstructure rested upon such foundations. Infidelity, materialism, and atheism find their vitality in the natural reaction from narrow restrictions, rigidly enforced by misdirected zeal.

The Christian economy being spiritual, the material appearance of the Christ was brief and local. Even His Apostles but dimly caught the significance of His mission, believing, as they evidently did, that He would return in the flesh during their lifetime and begin a temporal reign. The materialism of many sincere but misguided men still leads them to expect another "coming" in bodily form. Christ is all the time coming in the hearts of His spiritual followers, and such an advent is far more grand than any visible approach through the clouds with archangels and trumpets.

Jesus the Christ did not make use of the channels of traditional systems in His ministry, nor did He deal with problems of civil government or material progress. He touched the springs of life, but gave no direction as to the form of their activity. He formulated no system of theology, constructed no creed, and originated no plan for the preservation and dispensation of His own teachings. He was not a scientist, philosopher, nor an inventor; he sanctioned no particular system of education, and expressed no opinion

---

2. Case of Rev. Howard Macqueary.

upon the burning questions of the day. He was not even a reformer in the modern sense of that term. He began at the human centre, and not upon its circumference. He took little notice of those things upon which modern civilization is supposed to depend. He did not concern himself with different ethical systems, nor make any attempt to correct evils through improved legislation. His seed-sowing was below the surface of intellectual accomplishment, and its fruitage appears in motives rather than in forms of human life. He came to break bonds and open prison-houses; to relieve beating hearts from the pressure of artificial systems, ceremonies, and traditions, and to energize them with new life. He was unconventional in his tastes and habits, and in the choice of his social environment. When he came, religion had degenerated into a hollow mockery of ceremonial rites and rituals. He saw and condemned the hypocritical righteousness of the Pharisees, and exposed their spiritual deadness. He satirized their sanctimonious countenances, ostentatious fasts and alms, and their long and loud public prayers. The letter of religion had killed its spirit.

The Son of man came to teach men how to bring the spiritual realm into this life, without waiting to find it in the next. He showed that death did not consist in laying off the material body, but in dropping into a condition of animalism. He came to awaken man from a false dream of sense, to a consciousness of the Real, and to demonstrate that spirit is substance, and flesh only its shadow. The heavenly treasure is not bound, but its exuberant life overflows and fills every valley that is open to its crystalline current. How different from scholastic systems! Truth needs, not statement but embodiment. Men are inclined to feel that the proper place for God is in heaven, and that they, being upon earth, must be earthly, though they expect to be spiritual in the next world; but a correct theology cannot supply the place of unfolding eternal life.

"Though Christ a thousand times in Bethlehem be born,
　If He's not born in thee, thy soul is all forlorn."

The revelation of God through Nature is in full harmony with that which comes through the Son. Christ looked through the mantle of Nature and saw meanings, laws, and analogies which were invisible to those around him. He translated the spiritual significance of the sea, mountains, fields, trees, and vines, and through them interpreted truth "to his dull learners. The spontaneity and unstudied character of Christ's teachings, as shown in their natural childlike simplicity, was in strong contrast with the sophistry of intellectual logic. His illustrations and parables were as graceful as the opening of the leaves in Springtime. The unperverted type of the natural man, in his purity, as seen in Christ, confirms the inherent oneness of God and his children. If the image of God in man had not been marred, the whole race would now be in the same position as that which was occupied by "the last Adam." The beautiful proportions of the perfect human Model demonstrate that a full influx of the divine life tempers all the fancies of the imagination, and the impulses of the will, to a heavenly shaping. Christ and Nature reveal the same Father, but each on a different side. Jesus was a perfect man, because he was completely filled by the Christ-mind. "Till we all attain unto the unity of the faith, and of the knowledge of the Son of God, unto a full-grown man, unto the measure of the stature of the fulness of Christ."

That the Evangelists give no description of the personal appearance of Jesus is significant. By a uniform and deep intuitive sense of what was fitting, they delicately avoided any reference to his features, bearing, and personal appearance. For all such details we have only misty and doubtful tradition. The outer personality is veiled in the Scripture narratives. "The flesh profiteth nothing." The opaque shadows of outward shaping must be hid, else homage would be paid to "the letter."

The nature of the miracles of Christ is a theme which has been the occasion of much controversy. There has been cloudiness of interpretation and a lack of exact definition. A miracle is any wonderful event, but many limit it to events which they believe to be the result of some suspension or violation of natural law. Nature's laws are nothing more nor less than God's methods of action, and He does not contradict Himself. He who is "the same yesterday, to-day, and forever," is orderly in His manifestations. The miracle transcends the powers and experiences of the observer, and to him it is miraculous. But the observer is very limited in his knowledge, and has but an infantile comprehension of the beautiful regularity of the Father's operations. Telephonic communication for a distance of a hundred miles, or a sight of the "limited express," would, doubtless, have been a far greater wonder to Christ's auditors than any one of the miracles which he performed. There has been a long and bitter conflict upon the subject of miracles between pseudo-science and pseudo-religion, while, in fact, true science and real religion are in perfect accord. Each has occupied a false position, and thereby seen its supposed opponent in a false light. The scientist denies the existence of the supernatural in the sense of defining that which is special, or not uniformly the same under the same circumstances. So far he is correct, but his mistake is in limiting natural law to the material realm. Natural law loses none of its naturalness in the higher domains, and is no less uniform in its reign. On the other hand, the religious dogmatician draws a hard and sharp line between the natural and spiritual, and so fails to connect them. Unless the miracle transcends all law and order, it is no miracle to him. The battle of the knights over the question of the gold or silver shield illustrates the nature of the conflict. It is impossible for two truths to be in collision. God is the Author of Truth, and therefore in every realm it is sacred. Transactions which have seemed miraculous are losing that aspect just in proportion as knowledge of God and His methods broadens. Under an improved understanding of spiritual law in our own times, miracles of healing are becoming common. To that degree in which we make our wills plastic and at one with the Divine Will, we have God's power combined with our own, and His will is always good. Christ claimed no superior power to that possessed by his disciples, provided they were perfectly at one with the Father. "Greater things than I have done, ye shall do." He declared that all believers—those who come into an understanding of divine law—should exercise the same power that he did.

"That healing gift He lends to them
    Who use it in His name!
The power that filled His garment's hem
    Is evermore the same."

"These signs shall follow them that believe." If "them that believe" were limited to age, race, or condition, then would the word of the Lord be "bound." It is proper, however, that we exercise some discrimination in regard to the so-called miracles of the Bible. Those which have spiritual utility, and are in accord with the natural course of human progress, have everything in favor of their historic accuracy. Wonderful occurrences, which are beyond the evident range of such utility and naturalness, we may look upon as illustrative or allegorical. Miracles of mercy prompted by love and service have every element of reasonableness. Those like the arrested sun, Balaam's ass, and the story of Jonah, we can hesitate to accept in their literal sense, without in the slightest degree impairing the spiritual integrity of the Bible. A prominent evangelist once said that "if the story of Noah and the ark must go, the Gospels would go with it." A thousand times no! The living gospel has an infinitely broader foundation than any such transaction. Not that we need to deny that such events took place, but that we should disconnect them entirely from all that is vital and indispensable in Sacred Writ. Our reason is more directly God-given than the Scripture records. Touching this subject an eminent divine recently said, "If men persist in linking faith to a mechanical accuracy, historical criticism will overthrow that accuracy and faith together."

Did Jesus forgive sins? "And Jesus seeing their faith said unto the sick of the palsy; Son, be of good cheer; thy sins are forgiven." What is the forgiveness of sin? Not the remission of penalty, nor a suspension of the law that "whatsoever a man soweth, that shall he also reap." It is rather the putting away of sin, and only by and through that means, an escape from penalty. All the sin of the world is eternally forgiven by God. Our sins are unforgiven—to us—when we are unconscious of such forgiveness. Any one who can bring his brother into a consciousness of the divine forgiveness—forgives—brings pardon into manifestation. Forgiveness is the loving interpretation of the divine Mind by the Son. The sense of forgiveness awakened in the sinner kindles new love and life, and this turns him away from his sins, or rather, from his love of sinning. Following in the footsteps of the Son of God, any son of God may announce the divine pardon; that is, forgive. If forgiveness were not an eternal act on God's part, it would imply alteration in His Mind. So long as the human idea of God was that of a jealous Monarch, He was seen with human limitations. God is never less than perfect, so He cannot change His attitude. Our own imperfect states are reflected in the God of our consciousness, therefore we see what seems to be unforgiveness and even anger in Him. "For if ye forgive men their trespasses, your Heavenly Father will also forgive you." That temper of mind which forgives others their offences against us clarifies the spiritual vision so that God is seen in His true character of eternal Love and Pardon. The forgiving spirit characterizes the presence of the "Mind of Christ." The forgiveness of sin includes its abandonment. Not that we can, or would, be rid of its penalty; for that is disciplinary, in fact, indispensable. Discipline is beneficent because it destroys the love of sin. It is divine to forgive without limit. A recent writer[3] in commenting upon the false views of forgiveness and salvation which have grown up in the Church, says, "And as a means of escape from this unspeakable doom, she (the Church) has devised a doctrine of God's righteousness, and of the propitiation of its wrathful demands, which makes the sinner so much the subject of its 'scheme of grace' as to weaken his sense of responsibility, and deaden the consciousness of

---

3. Rev. L. C. Baker in *Words of Reconciliation* (Monthly), Philadelphia.

God within him as his power of recovery, so that salvation has come to be viewed as something done for him by proxy, and not wrought in him by the power of God. The idea of an imputed righteousness has supplanted that of personal righteousness as indispensable to salvation."

The great central and growing thought of the present time is, "The brotherhood of man." It is becoming clear that men cannot selfishly "save their own souls" out of relation with the salvation of others. The ties which bind the race into one bundle are divinely strong and close. That view of the visible Church which makes it an "ark of safety," or a salvation assurance society for the individual soul, is passing away. Christ came to light not only "the elect," but "every man that cometh into the world." Every child of God is a link in the great golden chain of His love. The harmonious vibrations of human progress, as divinely instituted, are from within, outward. Service is the active manifestation of the indwelling Christ. True service is not menial, but willing, joyous, spontaneous. As men live outside of self,—have their life in their fellows and in God,—the divine image in them is uncovered. The false ego of sensuous personality is lost, and the true self found. God is Love; and love is the giving out of good. The Son, being a perfect expression of the Father, gave His service, His life. Himself.

> "Love's power to give, grades what it can receive;
> Love that gives not, *is* not; it must bestow.
> And God is love; hence, going forth must know
> The power creative of itself; perceives
> In action only all that love can be.
> Who most can love, to him most love is given—
> Unmeasured love is all there is of heaven!"

The multitudes were filled, and had a surplus, from a few loaves and fishes; and so, good, given out, multiplies. The great soul is he that forgets that he has a soul, in his efforts for the salvation of others.

O glorious mystery of the Incarnation! Thou art a prophecy of that greater and general Incarnation when the "Christ-mind" will dwell in the whole brotherhood of humanity. O bright and joyous Christmas-time— never-ending Holy-day! Thou art a witness to the ever-recurring birth of the Prince of peace in the hearts of men.

VI. The Universality of Law.

> "Of Law, there can be no less acknowledged than that her seat is the bosom of God, her voice the harmony of the world; all things in heaven and earth do her homage, the very least as feeling her care, and the greatest as not exempted from her power."
>
> RICHARD HOOKER, 1553-1600.

WHAT IS the most important discovery of modern times? Some would answer, the art of printing, which, in its present marvellous stage of progress, scatters its winged pages "as thick as autumnal leaves that strow the brooks of Vallombrosa." Others would mention the wonderful utilization of steam, by the power of which the material forces of the world are a thousand times multiplied for the convenience and comfort of mankind. Still others would point to the unnumbered applications of electricity, the successive discoveries of which burst upon us almost as rapidly as its native flashes repeat themselves through the murky darkness of a summer evening thunder-storm. No; it is none of these. Of vaster moment than all these great achievements is the growing recognition of the fact that Law is universal.

What is Law? One eminent writer defines it as "an ascertained working sequence or constant order among the phenomena of Nature." Another calls it "the universal reign of a fixed order of things." Webster describes it as "any force, tendency, propension, or instinct, natural or acquired." Such definitions, though technically correct, are freighted with a cold, mechanical import which almost seems tinged with fatalism.

The theologian discourses upon Natural Law as a code of material legislation, infinite in detail, which, once for all, was put in force by the Deity, and then left to assert itself and punish its transgressors. Atheists and materialists, while admitting its orderly regularity within the physical domain, conceive it to be but the blind operation of inherent forces and tendencies.

Law is the uniform and orderly methods of the Immanent God. Natural Law, which pervades the material, mental, and spiritual kingdoms, is God in manifestation. But a short time ago, and the most intelligent observers limited the province of law to the more apparent operations of external nature. It was the prevailing opinion that the movement of the earth and other planets through space, the ebb and flow of tides, the growth of trees and plants, and the obvious multiform operations of gravitation and cohesion, mainly or wholly composed the realm of unvariable tendencies and courses of phenomena. Scientists regarded everything immaterial as beyond the pale of law; theologians looked upon the spiritual domain as above law, or supernatural; and the world in general believed in special providences and in every-day suspensions and variations in trains of orderly sequence. The most intelligent and reverent thought of the present day concedes the omnipotence and omnipresence of Law. If it be but another name for God in orderly manifestation, any lesser concept would dishonor and limit Him by the implication that He was self-contradictory and lawless.

"That very law which moulds a tear,
    And bids it trickle from its source,
That law preserves the earth a sphere,
    And guides the planets in their course."

There is no space, place, nor condition where there is exemption from Law's imperial dominion. The crystal dew-drop, the gentle zephyr, the shimmering wavelet, the fleecy cloud, and the resplendent sunset, all are just as they are by the mandate of Law. The graceful proportion and peculiar shade of every leaf, flower, plant, and tree are specified by Law. The rain, the cyclone, the earthquake, heat and cold, all scrupulously observe the Law. The fashion of the bird's wing and the insect's foot is regulated by Law. Plagues, pestilences, and famines come by Law. Orders of animals, birds, fishes, and reptiles appear upon the face of the earth, run their course, and disappear in accordance with the behests of Law.

But higher than these, man thinks, wills, imagines, and develops, mentally and spiritually by Law. Institutions, governments, civilizations, and religions, all owe their histories, peculiar development, and success or failure, to their relation to Law. Pain, joy, blessing, and all other kinds of consciousness, are ordained by Law. Even signs, wonders, and miracles are within its all-embracing boundaries, though the keen search of science may yet have failed to discover their footsteps.

Is, then, this all-comprehensive Law mechanical, merciless, tyrannical? Are we the helpless victims of a universal system, every detail of which is unavoidable and inevitable? No; not victims, but victors. While the discovery of the universality of Law" is the greatest human accomplishment of the nineteenth century, there is a kindred truth which even its closing decade has not brought into general recognition. It is the universal beneficence of Law. Law is infinitely intelligent, perfect, and beneficent. It requires more than a superficial glance at the subject to reach such a conclusion. It is a legal part of Law that friction, pain, and penalty shall result from its violation. Penalty is the shock that we feel when we come in collision with it. Speaking exactly. Law itself cannot be broken. If we transgress it, the Law remains intact, but we are broken. It is best that it should be so. If Law could in any degree be bent to conform to our variable wishes or standards, the moral and physical universe would become chaos. Penalty is not calamitous and from without, but rather inherent, subjective, corrective, and therefore good.

Even human statutory penalties for the violation of imperfect legislative codes are only intended to be corrective and preventive, both for the criminal and society. The vindictive element which formerly manifested itself in punative stripes and tortures—in the spirit of an eye for an eye—has largely passed away, except, perhaps, a lingering remnant in that form known as capital punishment.

Pain, whether physical, mental, or moral, is penalty, and comes from the bruises which we receive from avoidable collision with Law, but the Law itself sustains not the least fracture. It continues its smooth, harmonious course with out deflection or interruption.

Pain appears like an armed and vindictive enemy, but it is really a friend in disguise. If we look beneath its mask and recognize and accept it, it takes us by the hand and gently leads us back from the thorny thicket through which we are plunging at the behest of passion, ignorance, or weakness, into the smooth path which Law has made perfect for our resistless progress. Law is our judge, and pain the judgment. The cure for suffering is the recognition of its friendly mission, which makes its judgment accepted and confessed. When its beneficence is understood, and its errand interpreted, it becomes transformed into an angel of mercy. Paul's "thorn in the flesh" at length became a positive element of strength. If we struggle against penalty, and insist that it has been missent, or that it descends upon us from any outside source, it grows in intensity. Judgment denied, enforces its stern demands. If passion, animalism, and selfishness were not warned off and held in check by prospective penalty, how soon the otherwise beautiful human economy would become a wreck.

A correspondence of more profound depth and intensity is found in man's higher nature. The severe judgments of sin, materialism, and moral debasement are pain and remorse, mental and physical. These monitors rise up and eloquently appeal to men to turn about and come into harmony with Law. Judgment unheeded and defied at length becomes hell. While the old theological monstrosity of a God-made hell is a myth, we actually go to work and kindle hells of our own. When man's nature becomes disordered and perverted, the Law kindly incites a hellish condition to goad him, so that he may turn, and not forever drift away from the harmony of God and Law, and thus destroy himself. Hell is a necessity. Its punitive flames are fanned by heavenly love and beneficent law, and not by the anger of a wrathful Deity. The "consuming fire" purifies. If sin did not inevitably carry penalty on its back, men would keep on sinning forever. The greater the distance that the prodigal sons of God get away from Him in consciousness, the more intense the self-inflicted penalty which will finally turn their faces back towards the Father's house.

If Law be but a synonyme for God in outward expression, it is obvious that its economy is altogether wholesome. The perfection of Law shows an infinite breadth of both wisdom and love. Said Marcus Aurelius;—

> "All that is harmony for thee, O universe, is in harmony with me as well. Nothing that comes at the right time for thee is too early or too late for me. Everything is fruit to me that thy seasons bring, O nature. All things come of thee, have their being in thee, and return to thee."

It is only when our selfishness and ignorance foolishly antagonize the Law that to our distorted vision it seems baneful. Through dark and superstitious periods in the past, beneficent Law seemed so unfriendly that men erected it into a great evil Personality, and cringed in terror before it.

We may make Law our infinitely powerful ally. The man who utilizes steam or electricity in accordance with their own laws multiplies his physical accomplishment a thousand-fold. On the contrary, if he disregard their orderly methods, and strive to impose his own notional theories upon them, he will receive the judgment of penalty. As we render ourselves plastic to the healthful persuasions of Natural Law, and parallel her lines instead of crossing them, we enlist the potentiality of the universe in our service. Disregarding her, we "kick against the pricks," but through her cordial co-operation we may accomplish "all things." "Hitch your wagon to a star!" God's wise moral economy provides that His human children, made in His own image, should utilize His methods; and an intelligent recognition of this great boon makes man princely in power and Godlike in character. No longer being a slave to Law, he can—through her instrumentality—not only be free himself, but also command divine prerogatives and privileges.

But it will be objected, and with great plausibility, that there are natural laws which are hostile to man, and utterly beyond his control; as, for instance, those that produce earthquakes, tornadoes, and tempests, which often sweep physical humanity out of existence. From a material standpoint, these are evil, but the truth lies deeper. What is their significance, and what their relations to mankind? Convulsions of nature are throes, or growing pains, in the progressive development of the physical universe. The phenomena of cataclysms and deluges are but incidents in the great onward sweep of cosmic evolution.

As to their relations to man, they cannot harm him at any point. True, they may blot out his physical expression, but in reality that is no intrinsic part of him. From the "body" standpoint, material dissolution is the king of evils; but man is not body, and the physical point of view is false. Only by a general degradation is our flesh-consciousness identified with the ego; and it is this mistake, and only this, which clothes physical calamities with their terror. Reasoning from the basis of the real, evils can only be evils from their subjective moral quality. A stroke of lightning deprives a man of bodily expression. The *man* is intact. His means of material correspondence are removed; but morally he is no worse, and therefore no *evil* has befallen him. The change is in his relations and environment; not in himself, nor in his veritable I am, the consciousness of which forms his real being. That is a false and debased sense of *life* which makes it to consist of physical sensations. Such is animal life, but man is a "living soul." Only when we rise to the standpoint of the Real is our ordinary distorted view of that evolutionary step across an imaginary line called death clarified and corrected. The term evil is only applicable to a condition of subjective absence of good. None but thorough materialists can deny the validity of these premises and deductions. The beneficence of Law is, therefore, not disproved by any apparent hostility of what are known as the forces of Nature.

Plagues and pestilences result from violations of Law, or rather from the lack of recognition of the power and utility of higher laws with which man can ally himself to overcome and banish such calamities. While Natural Law is never suspended, there are mental and spiritual laws which rule and neutralize the power of those which are below, and man's divine sonship gives him dominion in the subordinate realm. One raises a pebble from the ground. Thus the law of gravitation is overcome by the higher law of the human will, though not for an instant is the earth's attraction lessened or suspended. Tree-life is superior to gravitation, and therefore the sap rises and overcomes it.

Spiritual laws occupy the highest rank in beneficence and potentiality, and, therefore, are primary and supreme among causative forces. The intellectual economy is inferior in rank, being expressive and resultant. The physical realm is a still cruder manifestation of the immaterial forces which have their source and play in unseen productive agencies. We speak of the "laws of matter," but matter has no laws of its own. It merely expresses the quality and shaping of what is back of and superior to itself. It is but a printed page, which has no meaning except as interpreted from beneath the letter.

Man must discern the fact that he is a sharer and an heir of the Divine Nature, and that with such an heritage he may assert his birthright of authority over the economies around and below him. He learns to govern, mould, and give quality to his own nature, and also to grasp and utilize the forces of the spiritual world from whence the innumerable lines of Law radiate and gather their potentiality. This knowledge, of itself, constitutes such a wonderful acquisition that the Christ affirmed that he that is least in the kingdom of heaven—the understanding of spiritual law—is greater than John the Baptist, who represented prophecy and morality. Even the least in the domain of the Real is of far more value than great accomplishment of inferior quality.

Noting the universality and beneficence of Law, and the transcendent importance and potency of Spiritual Law, it may be profitable to trace a few of its innumerable applications, and also to look at its relations with Providence, prayer, and freedom of the will.

Providence is within the limits of Law, and there can be no special providences unless there be special and capricious laws. A providential event may be as beneficent,—nay, more so,—if it come in an orderly manner, than if it were the outcome of partiality or lawlessness. If it were possible to bend Law to our notional desires instead of conforming ourselves to its infinitely wise shaping, the motive for such a chaotic act must be supreme selfishness. Shall man presume to change the universal order to accommodate the distorted partiality of his baser self? Can he improve upon Infinite Wisdom?

Whenever man's consciousness rises from the selfish animality which darkens the basement of his being, and looks out through the spiritual altitude of his nature, he instinctively feels the kindness of established order, and knows that "all is good." Law is not only supremely powerful, but it is ever waiting to serve us.

In view of the immutability of Law, what is the province of prayer? Is not any petition that would strive to change the divine order superfluous? If God's economy is *already* perfect, is it not an implication upon His wisdom to beg for its revision? The strained use of the prayer of petition for special material favors is standing evidence of the selfish materialism of humanity. If God be Infinite Love and Wisdom, and knows better what we need than we can know, how can we presume to counsel or enlighten Him? Can we ask even for needed spiritual blessing, expecting a change on His part in response? We misapprehend the nature of prayer. His Spirit is already omnipresent, awaiting our recognition, and how could it be more?

Is there, then, no place for prayer? Yes; for "prayer without ceasing." Prayer is communion, aspiration, oneness of spirit. It is soul-contact with the Parent-Mind, the reception of the Immanent God into the every-day consciousness. In its loftiest form it is a living recognition that the Infinite Love has already bestowed every possible gift, so that there is absolutely nothing to ask for. But there is unbounded utility in true prayer on the human side, to bring such a stupendous fact into our consciousness. As by such aspiration we come into oneness with God, we command a thousand-fold more blessing through spiritual law than would be possible if we possessed infinite power to bend the divine will, linked with our fallible wisdom to determine the manner of bestowment.

In proportion as men feel themselves to be "sons of God," they can wield divine forces and legally make them ministries of blessing. Take a case of physical ailment, for the recovery of which there are two possible forms of prayer. One, that God in answer to petition would change on His part so as to send forth a special influx of healing power. Such a response would imply changeableness, improvement, and existing imperfection on the part of God which our importunity would correct. The second, recognition that Unchangeable Good has already done everything necessary, and that it remains for us to come so close to Him as to be able to bring the divine ideal into outward expression, through and in accord with Law. A knowledge that physical wholeness is natural—as the external manifestation of spiritual forces already at our disposal—would powerfully aid in bringing lawful and potential wholeness into actuality. As "sons of God" we may learn to command orderly supernal powers, and through them to make visible such complete demonstrations as shall show answers to prayer from a Deity who is "without variableness or shadow of turning." Every possible prayer for what is truly the best is eternally answered, and the result is in readiness for us to bring into conscious manifestation. We need not beg good of a Father who is Infinite Love, but we must open our souls and quicken our spiritual vision to the perception of the infinitude of lawful gifts already our own. The grand mission of prayer is to bring us subjectively into harmony with God by the recognition of His presence in the soul. It is not a form of words, though it may be audibly expressed. In its essence it is loving intercourse with the Presence which besets our spirits "behind and before."

By infallible Law one grows into the likeness of his mental delineation of the Deity which he worships, for it forms his highest ideal of perfection. The more complete one's concept of God, the more divinely shaped will be his standards and attainments. To instruct or implore a God who is susceptible to change or improvement reflects its vacillation and imperfection upon the petitioner. The prayer of communion and aspiration unfolds the divine selfhood, and reveals the road to the utilization of Law, and the apprehension of truth, that through them men may acquire dominion which is princely in its richness. Such spiritual wealth is the natural heritage of "sons."

The universal cosmos, visible and invisible, has a rhythm, to discover the harmonious vibrations of which is man's high privilege and prerogative. Paul knew this when he affirmed, "I can do all things through Christ, which strengtheneth me." This was a reference, not merely to the historic Jesus, nor to any special bestowment of power, but to such a perception of God's orderly methods as enabled him to command them. These constitute the essential Christ which Jesus outwardly manifested.

Let us concisely state a few fundamental applications of Law that are of the highest importance and utility, but which humanity is slow to recognize.

Love is the high consummation and fulfilment of all Law. It casts out fear, discord, and imperfection. To minister is Godlike—Christlike. Giving out spiritual and material good fulfils divine order, and, therefore, benefits the giver as well as the recipient. In proportion to one's bestowment upon others his own being is enriched. Giving and receiving are found to be but the different sides of one whole. Ministry is the motive power of spiritual advancement; for the law of love reaches down, rules, and overcomes adverse laws which are below itself.

The laws of mental delineation are also of supreme importance in the human economy. "As a man thinketh in his heart, so is he." One unconsciously grows into the likeness of his favorite mental specifications, and finally becomes the expression of his ruling thought. Evil, if brought near, examined, and analyzed, grows more realistic as it is dwelt upon; and this is true even when the sincere purpose is its opposition. As darkness is the mere absence of light, so evil displaced by good fades to its native nothingness. Good is positive because it is Godlike and lawful. The objective vitality of evil is gained from the reflection of subjective consciousness. If we had nothing wrong in ourselves as a correspondence, we could never recognize the same quality in others; and if such a condition were general, the Christly law of non-resistance would have unlimited sway. "Thinketh no evil," is to give it no breathing space. Pessimism is unwholesome because it multiplies bad conditions and galvanizes them into life. One always finds what he looks for. Recognizing only the best in humanity, it is thereby subjectively and objectively emphasized and brought into manifestation. The sensational and realistic delineation of criminal details in journalism and fiction multiplies crime and criminals. One who commits a physical assault is speedily arrested and punished by society; but the assaults of dime novels, police-gazette literature and illustrations, upon youthful and plastic mind, are vastly more deadly. The exhibition and depiction of objective depravity arouse and stimulate its subjective correspondence.

"Vice is a monster of so frightful mien,
  As to be hated, needs but to be seen;
  Yet seen too oft, familiar with her face,
  We first endure, then pity, then embrace."

Nature is optimistic, and as civilization recedes from natural standards towards artificialness it tends toward chaos and decay. We may reverently affirm that God is perfect and infinite Optimism.

The throes and penalties which appear inherent in the material nature of man are the necessary incidents, experiences, and goads in the great process of spiritual evolution. Intrinsic growth in the individual and in society is through pain and confusion, these being the effervescence of good and evil,—the conflict between the divinity and the animality in dual human nature. The maledictions of the imprecatory psalms of David were directed against the adverse forces of his own lower nature, and not against foes without.

The immutable law of correspondence in physical expression would be of supreme utility to the race if its potency were generally recognized. The human body being but a literal transcript of the mind, physical inharmonies can be rectified through mental and spiritual lawfulness; but as the process is complex and gradual, the correspondence is not superficially apparent.

Those significant and well-defined laws which govern thought are also but lightly appreciated. Thoughts are powers, and even when unexpressed they go forth armed with influences for good or ill upon other minds. The moulding power of thought currents, and their utility or abuse as regulated by Law, are more truly corner-stones in the scientific Temple of Truth than are the orderly methods of gravitation, cohesion, or any other observed phenomena of the physical world. Large thought-space bestowed upon unworthy objects or propensities confers dominion upon them. Even an utter nonentity may thus crowd the whole field of vision, and be galvanized into supreme reality. The sensualist dwells in a sensual atmosphere, and to him the whole world has a corresponding hue. The whole objective universe takes on the color and quality of the subjective status of the beholder. If there be a barren waste within, the external world will be a veritable Sahara. All visible actions and occurrences are but the inevitable sequences of stored-up aggregations of thought. High thinking, cultivated and encouraged, elevates the consciousness and transforms the thinker. Thoughts being substance, each current delineation that is poured into the great reservoir of unconscious mind adds a tinge of its own color. Every sequence is not a matter of chance, but of Law.

Rich outward environment does not bring harmony and contentment, even though the world believes the reverse, as indicated by the mad race for power, wealth, and position. Material attainment, however marvellous, will never usher in the "Golden Age." The wealth of invention which has so wonderfully augmented man's physical accomplishment during the past fifty years has conferred no additional happiness. The greatly broadened scale of material comforts only increases and intensifies his sullen discontent with his lot. Humanitarians who confine their efforts to the amelioration of physical conditions alone, only touch the surface of human misery. If every one were housed in a palace, dissatisfaction, rivalry, and restlessness would still be the rule.

The intellect may be cultivated, and the tastes refined to the utmost, without in the least quickening the moral pulse or lifting man into a higher and more harmonious consciousness. When well-rounded spiritual and moral character becomes the goal of mankind, and the search for harmony is made within rather than without, ideal conditions will become manifest. By invariable Law the spiritual realm of man's nature is serene and perfect, and the ego must climb into its delectable atmosphere in order to inhale the divine ozone.

Everything that lives grows into the likeness of its environment. Man can invoke either the true or false, and surround himself with it as if by magic. By and through Law, he is a creator, and can build subjective worlds, and ere long the objective sphere takes on their quality. Materialistic science has fancied that it was exploring the whole realm of logical truth, while in fact it has hardly raised its eyes above the lower and cruder side. A study of the influence of unexpressed thought is as truly scientific as a research in microscopy or electricity; and the logical sequences of different subjective mental states are of far greater practical interest than an inquiry into the principles of chemistry or bacteriology.

A study of health is vastly more profitable than a study of disease, because every mental delineation presses for outward structural expression.

Religion teaches that Love is the sum total of the moral code, but science has yet to discover that Love is the grand focus where all the infinite lines of Law converge. It is already apparent to the spiritual vision of keen observers that Love is the highest Law; but the fact will gradually dawn upon humanity that in the kindgom of the Real, Love is the *only* Law. The law of attraction which is omnipresent in the material cosmos may be regarded as an exact correspondence of the universality of Love in the pure realm of all-embracing spirit. The colors of the rainbow, when blended, form the pure white light; and so, however complex and heterogeneous law in its thousand aspects may appear, its final translation is Love. In its ultimate. Love sees only love outside of itself. It finally becomes incapable of beholding anything besides, because all else is composed of subjective falsity. Only the Real will glorify the field of its delectable vision.

Tennyson beautifully expresses this thought:

"One God, one law, one element,
And one far-off, divine event,
To which the whole creation moves."

Love in its lower forms is educational. Personal, paternal, filial, and even conjugal loves are the training-schools of that broader, perfected, impersonal Law of Attraction. The grand climax of the welding of Law and Love will only be reached when it blossoms into universal recognition as the One Force of the Universe. Then will be realized the *scientific* exactness of the declaration that "God is Love." Such a subjective recognition, whether here or hereafter, is known as Heaven.

"Where good and ill,
 And joy and moan,
 Melt into one,
There Past, Present, Future, shoot
Triple blossoms from one root;
 Substances at base divided
 In their summits are united;
There the holy essence rolls.
 One, through separated souls."

All lesser and lower conditions lack perfect law*fulness*, and are but mirror-like reflections of different degrees of unlawful consciousness. All other characteristics ascribed to God are subjective images projected and magnified. The "consuming fire" of pure Love may wear a terrible aspect to those who are persistently law-less, and that aspect is called hell. Such distorted vision kindles purifying internal fires until falsity is consumed, and this brings God—the Real—into recognition as "All in all."

VII. The Solidarity of the Race.

Conscious life consists of relations. The human economy is like a great tree, the branches and leaves of which—all springing from one root and nourished by the same sap—spread themselves forth that they may feel the glow of the sunlight. Life is a continuous divine communication. While it appears broken into a vast number of disjointed fragments, there is but One Life. It is the material and false sense of life which gives it the aspect of independent units. The true life is a derived, shared, and related consciousness. Without any loss of individual responsibility, each one belongs to the race, which as a whole would be incomplete without him. Life to each seems finited and separated in himself. He thinks of his being as distinct, having its own basis, development, interests, and objects, all within a well-defined boundary.

But life is so interwoven with life—or rather is so truly a part of the One Life—that an individual is like a bit of color in a great mosaic.

The ultimate acme of humanity is universal brotherhood. This will not be attained by means of any new departure in sociology, perfected legislation, nor ideal political economy, but from a higher consciousness which will fuse and unify heart and character. The current of spiritual life flows from the centre outwards, carrying on its bosom rich offerings of loving service and ministry. The cold tide of selfishness, which ebbs from without inward, ends in a deadly vortex, because it has no compensating outflow.

Individual man does not think for himself. He is taken up and borne along by great thought currents in which he is submerged. While he has a feeling of independence, he is as conditioned as a piece of drift-wood in the rapids of a mighty river. The great sweep of events and developments brings to the surface its successive exponents, but these seeming rulers of the movement are but its incidental expressions. Every great wave of human thought, whether social, political, or religious, bears upon its crest a few leaders upon whom the movement seems to depend; but in reality they are swept along in the prevailing current. In the eleventh, twelfth, and thirteenth centuries the temper of Europe was ripe for the Crusades, otherwise the instigators of those great incursions never could have inspired the vast waves of humanity, which, under the banner of the cross, surged eastward for the recovery of the Holy Sepulchre. Luther was but the instrumental articulation of the spirit of the ripening evolution of religious liberty of the Renaissance. In the fifteenth century Europe began to feel—even though unconsciously— the presence of a great western continent, and this blind apprehension became incarnate in Columbus. All great distinctive mental currents find special embodiment; therefore, personal leadership is the outcome rather than the inspiration of great transitions. The general character of great mental currents may be tempered and modified by commanding spirits if their main trend be respected; but oftener apparent leadership is an adroit utilization of existing cumulative forces. The world was just at that stage of religious progress that was fitted for Calvin when he appeared; and when its thought had advanced from stern "decrees" towards "free grace" Wesley came upon the stage and gave it formal expression. It would be as easy to transplant the customs, manners, and modes of communication of Calvin's time into the present era as to find a fit place for his theological thought; and yet there are those who would patch up that musty doctrinal fabric for present use.

The great ocean of human mind rises and falls, ebbs and flows, in huge waves and not in detached drops. Men are unconsciously bound together by a thousand ties, real though intangible. The thunder of the rhythmic march of the mass drowns the light footfalls of those who mark an independent time.

Should we, then, be discouraged in our efforts for individual advancement? Does the deafening diapason of the multitude render all finer melody impracticable? No; for in a sense every man is the race. While in the lower realm of mind, personalities are mainly expressive, in the higher, individual attainment is race potentiality. The very foremost member in his progress towards the divine human ideal, represents a veritable race achievement.

Our ideas of human brotherhood are often limited to the present generation; but it includes all who have gone before, and all who will come after. Without affirming the doctrine of metempsychosis, or re-incarnation, there is a sense in which we have lived before the present life. Forms of life come and go; but life in its essence, being in and of God, is without beginning or ending. We shall be spiritually intertwined and incarnated in those yet to come. The race, past, present, and future, is one organism. For it, as weell as ourselves, we are thinking, willing, acting, and loving. The Scriptures teach that the fathers still live in the children, and that their transgressions, and still more their attainments, are shared by them, and science confirms the statement. Rightly understood, the seeming hard law of "the survival of the fittest" is found to be beneficent, for the fittest are channels of blessing to those who are less fit. As clear life-giving streams flow down the mountain sides, and refresh and make fertile the meadows below, so lofty human attainment, towering above the low plane of sensuality and materialism, helps to lift up and spiritualize the whole race-life. Service reaches clown to the things below. It is difficult to help those who are upon our own plane from lack of vantage ground.

The working field for the promotion of the evolution of the spiritual life is as broad as humanity, and reaches all generations. Jesus, who expressed the essential Christ, said, "I, if I be lifted up from the earth" (that which is material and selfish) "will draw all men unto me."

Human personality has been so deeply engaged in working out its *own* salvation, that it has overlooked its organic relations. Dogmatic theology has iterated and reiterated the injunction, "Save your own soul;" but the most ideal salvation is the forgetfulness of the "own soul" in devotion to the general soul. The very essence of salvation is the death of selfishness. Humanity is bound in one bundle, therefore its kinships and relations are of primary interest. In a sense we incarnate ourselves in those around us. Aristotle defined a friend as "one soul in two bodies."

The spiritual victories gained on this arena of life, and renewed, generation by generation, are grand in their scope and significance. We wrestle with principalities and powers, and that in the presence of a cloud of interested witnesses. The sorrows and trials of one are those of all, and the triumphs of each are a general inspiration. If the soul-currents do not flow from within outwards they become stagnant. Dogmatic theology which conceives of salvation as a "plan," has largely lost the consciousness of that "bond of the spirit" which held the primitive church in a loving fellowship. In the parable of the sheep and the goats, Jesus taught that character and ministry, and not creed, formed the basis for the heavenly condition. No man liveth to himself, and no man dieth to himself. The ever-widening circles of a personal consciousness of the presence of the divine image within, go out like waves to refresh the whole human family of God.

Selfish attempts at soul-saving through the efficacy of ordinances, rituals, and sacraments, rather than through intrinsic character, have narrowed and chilled the influence of the Church, and rendered it artificial and unattractive. Man's spiritual ideal is to be a channel through which the divine life and love may flow out to his fellows. "Sons of God" are those who are crucified in the lower self, and from the high altitude of their resurrection are able to draw men unto them.

That evolutionary step called death does not interrupt nor set aside the great vital current of race-progress and unity. Being members one of another, the ties of common interest and destiny stretch out both backwards and forwards. Life is one, and so-called death is but an incident. The spiritual world is as truly here as in a future condition. The vital test is not time nor location, but moral quality. Has the spiritual man—"the mind of Christ"— gained the ascendency? Paul in speaking of his tribulations affirms that he was being "baptized for the dead." We suffer from limitations and burdens which past generations, through the channel of ancestral life, have imposed upon us. In like manner the present generation is engaged in a hand-to-hand conflict, not merely for itself, but for a coming brotherhood, even down to the distant eons of the future. The keen spiritual perception of Paul enabled him to see the great environing "cloud of witnesses" which view with absorbing interest every step of our advance. Could our dull vision be clarified so that we might catch a glimpse of that great host, what an inspiration it would lend!

Christ conquered everything which is adverse to the race, and his victory was its triumph. He uncovered the "image of God" which had been buried by traditional rubbish and sensuous materialism. The conquest of the Head is the conquest of every member. Every brother in whom the Christly nature becomes incarnated gives an upward impulse along all the innumerable lines which radiate from him as a centre. He is a saviour who breaks the captive's chains, takes off the shackles, opens prison doors, and proclaims freedom. The great human campaign will not be ended until every member of the race has been translated into a "son of God." He is already that except in manifestation. The unmanifested who have passed on before have a vicarious interest in us and in our achievements. Each needs a "God-speed" and a drawing upwards.

While man stands at the apex of the great pyramid of sentient life, he is yet in bondage to his lower nature. His goal is a deliverance into perfect spiritual liberty.

It is supposed that heredity brings evil as well as good; but evil being negative, and having no God-like basis in the real, loses its vitality by the "third or fourth generation," while good goes on even to the thousandth.

The healing streams of altruism run out until they lose themselves in the ocean of eternal love. Race solidarity makes it a privilege for the strong to carry the burdens of the weak until they are finally rolled off. Therefore brotherly limitations will be overcome by brotherly aid. Man cannot live to himself, because he is crystallized into a great organic unity.

"Be noble! and the nobleness that lies
In other men, sleeping but never dead,
Will rise in majesty to meet thine own."

Missionary effort among the heathen will largely be barren so long as they are taught that there is an inseparable wall between them and their ancestral dead. Their views of the solidarity of interest between themselves and other generations, in many cases, are in advance of so-called Christian nations. A reasonable and practical spiritual religion, which would recognize the loving fellowship which binds them to their kindred who have gone before, would powerfully appeal to the "divine image" which is latent in every darkened heathen soul. God's ultimate economy in humanity is to bring it together, and its lines of reconciliation converge in Him. The comprehensive love which unifies divinity and humanity is the great law which includes all other laws.

How to reconcile the frictions of society is a problem which is attracting the attention of the civilized world. In the past there has been a wider variation in the material conditions of the human family than to-day, but never before has there appeared such a general restlessness. There is a universal reaching out for improvement. Blind and mistaken efforts to bring it about consist partially in organized antagonisms. Classes, trades, and sections solidify, in order to oppose other classes, trades, and sections, and believe that they are conserving their best interests. It is forgotten that society is an organism, and that all its members cannot perform the same kind of service. The perfect human body is a unit; but the office of each member is unlike that of every other, and therein is completeness. "When one member suffers all suffer."

Socialism is a term which is used with a great variety of meaning. To some it signifies—at least as an ultimate accomplishment—a forcible division of all material wealth by law and coercion. To others it mainly comprises an increased assumption of productive agencies, business operations, and wealth distribution by the State, including a steady enlargement of governmental functions in the future. But true socialism must begin from within, and have its basis in unselfish character. The spirit of love and altruism must be cultivated and awakened until it becomes prevailing, and as rapidly as this takes place its legitimate fruits will be outwardly manifest. Any socialism which contains elements of jealousy, avarice, or coercion is a counterfeit. Any forcible interference with the natural laws of wealth-distribution would discourage thrift and industry, conduce to idleness, and stimulate avarice and anarchy. If through any ostensible legalized process men can get what they do not earn, production will be diminished and decay ensue. Many well-meaning philanthropists confine their attention almost entirely to material conditions, while the royal road to improvement is only through better moral conditions. That sin, intemperance, and improvidence bring forth their inevitable fruit of poverty, misery, and suffering, is not the fault of our social system. Causation lies deeper. The most helpful help which can be given is to teach men, through character re-enforcement, how to help themselves. It is not a division of "silver and gold" that is needed; for even if that were practicable it would at once diminish production, raise the price of all necessities, and chill industry and progress. The ills of society are directly attributable to the lack of unselfishness, love, and character education. The time is not distant when these will be regarded as of far greater value than material wealth. As a basis for happiness, money is the most disappointing thing in the world. Let a truer estimate prevail. Great wealth pursued as an end is a curse to any member of the human family. There is no such soul-dwarfing, hell-inciting, suicidal occupation on earth as the selfish piling-up of surplus wealth as the object of life. The possessor of millions who goes on adding to his store, as a gratification of his insane ambition to accumulate, and lives without a conscientious regard for his obligation to his fellow-men, is surely kindling within himself that torment which Dives experienced, because he is defying the supreme law of his nature. Beneath all the golden glamour, such an one, in the truest sense, is blind and naked and sick and in prison. It is not the fact of the millions, for money is useful, but that their selfish possession will eventuate in a self-made hell in the human soul. Heaven and hell are not places, but conditions of character. They are legitimate harvests that come from diverse kinds of seed-sowing. Better a free soul as a digger of ditches, than one which is enslaved by its wealth. Such an one is like a bee submerged in its own honey. Bion once said of a niggardly rich man, "That man does not own his estate, but his estate owns him."

The millennium will consist of the reign of love and unselfishness. Improved economic theory and legislation are powerless to bring it into manifestation. Education in the ordinary sense is also utterly unable to bring about moral reform. Only as human consciousness is lifted into the spiritual zone and the "image of God" uncovered, will that harmony and wholeness be realized which is able to transform the earth into a paradise.

The manifestation of the intrinsic brotherhood is hindered and chilled by the conventionalities of our modern civilization. The deep fountains of human love and sympathy are sealed, and artificial barriers are built up between souls. A code of formal precedents, rules, and maxims becomes the unwritten, though inviolable law of society, which is based upon selfishness and worldly policy. Each soul wears a polished armor, which, though invisible, is as cold and impenetrable as steel, and nothing less than the manifested law of love in a general glow can ever melt it away. Man mistakenly considers himself a unit, and still inquires if he is his "brother's keeper." He has not yet drained the cup of self-sacrifice and discovered the sweetness which is hid at the bottom. Such an accomplished ideal would bring heaven into earth-life and emancipate humanity from the slavish ties of the lower self.

The law of ministry is not merely moral, but it is scientific. It constitutes the broad highway to racial and ideal harmony. The observance of fundamental law is a privilege rather than a duty, for it carries rich reward. "He that loveth his life loseth it, and he that hateth his life in this world shall keep it unto life eternal." Opportunity for service is a boon conferred. In the human economy it seems almost necessary that some cups should be empty, in order that there may be room for the overflow of others, so that both can enjoy their sweetness. If all were filled just to the brim, where could any room be found for the exercise of the privilege of bestowment?

The divine life consists of infinite ministration. Jesus expressed its dominion in the loving service of "washing the disciples' feet." Here the whole policy of the world is reversed. Only love can interpret love. "Except as ye become as little children," judged by conventional standards, seems like weakness and foolishness. Forms and traditions which have encased us with their worldly wisdom must be torn away before the tendrils of our being can be free to cling in graceful embrace to neighboring souls. The higher life is not a refinement. It is the awakening of a new consciousness—the glow of the divine image within.

The new brotherhood rises above the altitude of ethical rules and obligations. There is no search for the boundary-line between justice and injustice, for balanced obligations are left behind. The very conditions of inequality furnish vantage-ground for both a divine and human overflowing, which will continue until disconnected and stagnant pools are unified and swallowed up in a common sea of living interest and destiny. The two grand divisions of right and wrong will be superseded by those of the loving and the unloving, until at length the hardness of the latter will be melted away. The mighty law of love will finally submerge all its inferiors.

The racial soul is the grand unit, and all share its experiences and live its life. However dissimilar the initiates, each travels the grand highway, and passes through the same cycles of spiritual unfoldment. The great racial consciousness is being solidified by the cement of love. Seeming inequalities find their interpretation in the fact that the vicarious principle runs through the warp and woof of the whole human fabric. The innocent suffer in the penalties of the guilty, and the sinful share in the warm glow which is kindled by the loving.

But the perfect unity of racial mind exists only in the higher or the spiritual realm. Above the great equatorial line which separates it from that which is sensuous, peace and oneness are perfected. In the lower hemisphere is found the temporary, the seeming, the material, the delusive. It is the abode of shadows. The human ego abides with them until, through the discipline of penalty and "growing pains," it emerges into the higher realm of the One Mind. Here the grind and the friction of the baser zone are unknown. Here in the sunshine of the Kingdom of the Real, the upper branches of the great human tree blossom and produce their fruit. Here men are one because they are united in God. Humanity ultimates in the universal soul. Here is the final wielding of eternal Fatherhood, sonship, and brotherhood. Every heartthrob of the Divine Father sends the vital current of love and unity coursing through the veins of the remotest member.

Mankind is of one coinage, for all bear the divine image. This makes the lowest semblance of humanity lovely. Though yet unmanifested, he is a son of God. We are instructed to love our neighbor as ourselves, but the Christly standard is still higher. "Love your enemies." But there are no "enemies," for they have been transformed. As our eyes are opened the divine image shines through all human wrappings.

VIII. Man's Dual Nature.

THE HUMAN economy includes two distinct selves. The baser of these in reality is but a seeming, a claimant; but it may be more convenient to consider its pretensions as having a real basis, which they assuredly possess to the eye of material sense. The senses and the sensuous mind constantly pour in testimony favorable to the assumptions of the illusive ego. The spiritual perception, whose voice in the great human majority is so faint as to be almost inaudible, brings into the consciousness the true ego in just that degree of clearness which past unfoldment has enabled it to reach. The material self, while not necessarily vile—as measured by outward ethical moral standards —if dominant, is selfish, delusive, and of the earth, ea In view of such a fact, it is quite satisfactory to find that it *is* a claimant rather than the intrinsic reality. Jesus, who through his personality com manifested the divine self, declared, "It is the spirit that quickeneth; profiteth nothing." The human spiritual ego is in at-one-ment with mind, and therefore divine in its nature and characteristics.

In the early history of the race we find only the animal man mere sensuous knowledge, and destitute of spiritual consci aspiration. Physical sensation, pleasurable or painful, comp total of his knowledge and experience. His life consisted of sensuous gratification, and all his energies were put forth upon that plane.

The animal instinct of defence of self, offspring, and friends, led to rudimentary organization, and at length to barbaric social conditions. Patriarchal, tribal, and in process of time still broader forms of government, resulted; and finally ideas of justice and equity were evolved by slow and painful processes. Material development and civilization came in due time, with a gradual unfoldment of the intellectual faculty. By a slow and almost imperceptible transition there dawned upon the fittest, perceptions of the unseen, concepts of a spiritual self, and hopes of future immaterial existence.

The earlier consciousness was only of the body, but there came a gradual evolution of the idea of body and spirit. The former was regarded as far more substantial than the latter, and such is the state of consciousness in which the great majority of the human family are living at the present time.

e coming and ideal state of development—the dawn of which is already
ding its soft light abroad—is a spiritual consciousness, of which the body
a visible expression. The senses will lose their supremacy, and their
be discredited, and then it will be found that spirit is the veritable
e ego; and this when applied to the present state of existence as
which is in the future. The higher self is not a refinement of the
the quickening and germination of a divinely planted seed.
ot be gilded, whitened, nor refined. It cannot rise above
vn Kingdom. There is a new generation,—a birth from
itself in the enthronement of a new consciousness,
assed away, and all things have become new."
tive recognition of God, and of its intrinsic
s within and beholds God's image, and that
te acquaintance with his Maker. Viewed
explained and confirmed. God cannot
ctive, whether Bible, Church, creed,
us in opening the spiritual eyes.

VIII. Man's Dual Nature.

THE HUMAN economy includes two distinct selves. The baser of these in reality is but a seeming, a claimant; but it may be more convenient to consider its pretensions as having a real basis, which they assuredly possess to the eye of material sense. The senses and the sensuous mind constantly pour in testimony favorable to the assumptions of the illusive ego. The spiritual perception, whose voice in the great human majority is so faint as to be almost inaudible, brings into the consciousness the true ego in just that degree of clearness which past unfoldment has enabled it to reach. The material self, while not necessarily vile—as measured by outward ethical or moral standards —if dominant, is selfish, delusive, and of the earth, earthy. In view of such a fact, it is quite satisfactory to find that it *is* a claimant only, rather than the intrinsic reality. Jesus, who through his personality completely manifested the divine self, declared, "It is the spirit that quickeneth; the flesh profiteth nothing." The human spiritual ego is in at-one-ment with the Christ mind, and therefore divine in its nature and characteristics.

In the early history of the race we find only the animal man, possessing mere sensuous knowledge, and destitute of spiritual consciousness and aspiration. Physical sensation, pleasurable or painful, comprised the sum total of his knowledge and experience. His life consisted of sensuous gratification, and all his energies were put forth upon that plane.

The animal instinct of defence of self, offspring, and friends, led to rudimentary organization, and at length to barbaric social conditions. Patriarchal, tribal, and in process of time still broader forms of government, resulted; and finally ideas of justice and equity were evolved by slow and painful processes. Material development and civilization came in due time, with a gradual unfoldment of the intellectual faculty. By a slow and almost imperceptible transition there dawned upon the fittest, perceptions of the unseen, concepts of a spiritual self, and hopes of future immaterial existence.

The earlier consciousness was only of the body, but there came a gradual evolution of the idea of body and spirit. The former was regarded as far more substantial than the latter, and such is the state of consciousness in which the great majority of the human family are living at the present time. The coming and ideal state of development—the dawn of which is already shedding its soft light abroad—is a spiritual consciousness, of which the body is only a visible expression. The senses will lose their supremacy, and their evidence be discredited, and then it will be found that spirit is the veritable and concrete ego; and this when applied to the present state of existence as well as to that which is in the future. The higher self is not a refinement of the lower, but rather the quickening and germination of a divinely planted seed. The old nature cannot be gilded, whitened, nor refined. It cannot rise above the boundary of its own Kingdom. There is a new generation,—a birth from above,—and it manifests itself in the enthronement of a new consciousness, "Behold old things have passed away, and all things have become new." The soul comes into a subjective recognition of God, and of its intrinsic oneness with Him. The man looks within and beholds God's image, and that constitutes his first real and intimate acquaintance with his Maker. Viewed philosophically he finds this identity explained and confirmed. God cannot be apprehended through anything objective, whether Bible, Church, creed, or ordinance, though these may be aids in opening the spiritual eyes.

When the inner vision is clarified, and the transfer of the conscious ego takes place, the soul is surprised and delighted in its new relations, and with Thomas it exclaims, "My Lord and my God."

Stated scientifically. Law is God in universal manifestation. The evolution of the spiritual self is a gradual and painful process to sensuous experience; for as the spiritual self is developed, the sensuous man—or rather his dominion—is dying by inches. Paul declared, "I die daily." The aggressiveness and expansiveness of the divine self have been well illustrated by the "leaven," and by the quickening of the life-germ in a grain of mustard-seed.

So long as the spiritual ego remains latent, the baser self is content to travel the horizontal road of sensuous existence with a more or less active intellectual accompaniment. But at length the jar of a stroke of affliction, or experience of some reverse of fortune, awakens the spiritual ego, and from that time an irrepressible conflict begins. Then the lower self may cry, peace! peace! but there is no peace. The contest for supremacy has opened, and sooner or later it will rage with great intensity. Sometimes a temporary anodyne is administered through the observance of formal creeds, sacraments, and rituals, but ere long their unsubstantial nature is brought to light. The "carnal man" is willing to be refined, to be moral, and even religious, but is not willing to abdicate the throne. In a variety of armors and disguises he disputes every inch of the ground, over and over again. Paul gives many graphic descriptions of his own experience in this warfare. "Even we ourselves groan within ourselves, waiting for our adoption; to wit, the redemption of our body." He also speaks of the body as being presented "a living sacrifice."

Some time in every one's experience the fact is brought home to him with startling emphasis, that his foes are "those of his own household." Outside enemies are feeble and puny when compared with those that are intrenched within. While they lack the intrinsic reality of a divine basis, to the subjective consciousness they are an armed and malignant host.

Man must pay the penalty for his mistakes, even though he make them through ignorance. He finds to his cost that he has taken the unreal to be real, and counted shadows as substances. He lives so thoroughly in the body, with its selfish passions, feelings, and inclinations, that they fill his field of vision, and seem to be himself. These experiences, though so vivid, have only the basis of a material dream. The selfhood is in a state of inversion. The real ego is smothered and buried until it passes into temporary oblivion.

The Adamic pretension must be disallowed, and "the mind of Christ" put on. The former is the "carnal mind" which is "at enmity with God," and the latter is God manifested in us. The first embraces the material Kingdom wherein is tribulation, and the second is the internal and immortal man which "cannot sin." The carnal is built up into a great structure composed of self-illusions, deceptions, race opinions, fears, and errors, into which we have been born, and by which we are environed; the spiritual is the Kingdom of Heaven "which is within you." The former is the life which is to be laid down or "lost" in order to the saving of the latter, which is the true immortal self. The first is the "natural man" to whom spiritual things are "foolishness," and the last is God-consciousness in the soul, or a realized at-one-ment with the Divine Fatherhood.

Man has two lives, two minds, two memories, and a double consciousness. He has an internal and an external nature. He has looked everywhere outside of himself for God, while he can only truly gaze upon the Father by beholding His image within. When he first feels the persuasive influences of the divine self, he finds that it gently woos his steps directly away from or *across* his former inclinations. This brings before him a cross which though heavy must be borne. So long as he tries to follow both leadings, or alternates between them, he is crucified. This will continue until the "old man" is put off and the spiritual centre illumined, and then the cross fades out and the crown appears in its place. The promised "new heavens and new earth" are not external phenomena, but are new illuminations within the spiritual self.

Many conscientious souls fail to recognize their duality, and therefore live in bondage to the sensuous nature. They observe external morality, but practically their ego is the material self. They are, therefore, subject to all the turmoil, disease, and restlessness that prevail upon the plane upon which they dwell. They look for their "heaven" only in a future state, and expect it as a reward, bestowed through substitution. Thus the spiritual self remains year after year in an embryotic, or at best a rudimentary state. The divine ego all the while contains the germs of wholeness, harmony, love, and peace; but the mistaken consciousness is groping in the basement beneath it. How can the ascent be made, in order that the abode of spiritual sunshine may be reached? By inward aspiration and a settled non-recognition of all that is not divine and spiritual. By steadily gazing upward in thought, as well as in performing external duty, and by shutting evil and negation out of the field of vision. Look within for God, rather than towards a faraway heaven. Think of Him as Infinite Life, Love, and Truth, rather than as an imperial Ruler upon a throne. Let positive oneness and harmony with Him grow and glow in the consciousness. This is grasping the higher selfhood. "As a man thinketh in his heart so is he." He can change his whole moral complexion by the transforming power of thought. Holding God in the consciousness is "Godliness which is great gain." Obedience to divine commands, as coming from a source outside, has in itself little transforming energy. We are possessed by that which we dwell upon, and give large thought-space to that which we love.

The world, and even the church, have been accustomed to associate the spiritual consciousness mainly, and often almost wholly, with the next state of existence; but it should be a present experience and life. Our mentality is so crowded with shadowy externalities that no personal consciousness builds up the selfhood of the higher life. True spirituality is composed of nothing ghostly, nor of that which is thrust upon us after the breath leaves the body, but its essence is present life and love. The act of laying off the physical expression does not change the spiritual character. The higher consciousness is the atmosphere from whence the ego draws its nourishment, both here and hereafter. It is the influx of the overflowing divine vitality, and comprises the realm of eternal substance and reality. If the material part were practically regarded as the shell or the husk, all would be well; for shells and husks are useful in their places, but not wholesome for subsistence.

It is our high privilege to luxuriate in the beauty and sunshine of the spiritual world now. As the ego of the higher life is unfolded, it attracts that which is like itself, and builds its own delectable environment. All our vitality comes through the divine self, even though we are unconscious of its reception. That which is inner finally expresses itself in ultimates. It is the substance of all our strength, health, virtue, and life. As the lungs form the channel for the reception of the oxygen and ozone from the atmosphere, so the spiritual selfhood receives the rich flood of divine life and truth with which the whole unseen universe is surcharged. The Adamic self is as unable to cognize the waves of spiritual influx as is the ear to see, or the eye to hear.

Both the silent and expressed recognition of the divine selfhood in others aids them in bringing it into manifestation. The idealization of our brothers and neighbors as divine egos, while we close our eyes to their lower selfhood and its imperfections, helps to lift them into the real and the ideal.

The higher and lower planes are never mingled nor confused, for there is a "great gulf" between them. The character of the first Adam is fixed. He is the abode of sin, discord, and death. His mind as well as body is honeycombed with mortality. He has physical sensation, but no real life. He is playing a part and acting a character.

True life comes through openness toward God. The traditional far-away God is not a "Present Help." The fact must come into human consciousness that the soul is in God, and God is in it. Dwelling with such a Presence the world becomes a living Theophany, the soul substantial rather than the body, and nature so transformed that it seems ready to melt into spirit. Character is a solid entity, while wealth, power, and pleasure are ephemeral appearances. Communion with heaven is through inward states, and not by way of tidings and messages from without. We are not souls imprisoned in fleshly tabernacles, but egos possessing powers of expression from within and without. The highest proof of immortality comes not from external evidence, reason, or analysis, but from the fact that man can become thoroughly emancipated from the dominion of the body while still using it. "Our conversation is in heaven;" and that is an internal spiritual life and illumination, rather than a distant locality.

"Take no thought for your body." Our ills come from our subservience to its demands, appetites, pride, and delusive selfhood. It is well in its secondary place, as expression; but when it holds the chief place it becomes an unrelenting tyrant. It will pursue and persecute the fettered soul until the higher part, re-enforced by divine consciousness and oneness, turns and achieves a spiritual victory.

The "last Adam," being in the divine image, is already perfect, and cannot know change or improvement. The false claimant which believes itself to be the ego is the abode of sin and all inharmony. The dominant sense being untruthful reflects its own likeness as in a mirror. To improve the reflection we do not manipulate the glass, but change the object which is reflected. As man begins to feel himself spirit instead of body he grows into spiritual conditions. Here is the whole basis of spiritual healing, both as practised in the primitive church and since that time. Healing is simply improved spiritual consciousness outwardly manifested. That religion which makes salvation a plan, creed, sacrament, or substitution, cannot heal, because the physical rather than the spiritual consciousness remains present and ruling. It is not merely the fact that men outwardly are overt sinners, but that they dwell upon the plane of materiality. So long as this continues they will remain in the meshes of its correspondence and subjugation. This is the climate where the damps, miasmas, blights, and disorders of the external world live, move, and have their dominion.

Man has concerned himself but little with the quality of his thoughts, but has been greatly distressed by the phenomena which they directly produce.

The infinite utility of spiritual consciousness in shaping expression has hardly yet dawned upon the human understanding. Man has not claimed and manifested the good, because he has thought of himself as "a poor sinful creature," and believed that the good did not belong to him. He has felt that his own little life and ego were independent and not a part of the One Mind and Life, and so has unwittingly shut himself away from the stream of divine involution.

The lower ego sees evil in the light of an entity, and even in the form of a malignant Personality; and therefore the consciousness, from pre-occupation, has no room for the spiritual allness of Infinite Good. There is an appearance of two great opposing principles, and therefore a divided allegiance. This delusion is reflected outward in all directions. Reaching the altitude of the understanding that spirit is the only vital reality, man can be absent from the discords and illusions of the world of sense, even though yet in the midst of them.

Paul declares that "the mind of the flesh" (the baser selfhood) "is not subject to the law of God, neither, indeed, can be." It is this seeming personality that fears God even though He be Love. If heaven were a locality it would be no other than veritable hell to any persistently base and selfish soul that might be shut up within its confines. This structure of concrete selfishness, which is the seeming I, may well fear the "consuming fire." While the real man cannot be harmed, it will consume that which men feel to be themselves, and therefore they suffer from fear of destruction.

Love, to this "old man" has a terrible aspect, because, as a bundle of carnal tastes, pursuits, and appetites, he instinctively feels that it is his omnipotent enemy. The veritable divine self is ever young and indestructible, but the conscious ego fails to identify itself with it. Paul in his Epistle to the Hebrews declares that "those things which are not shaken may remain." The sin and death in man invite the purifying flames, but he (the intrinsic self) will not be subject to their fury. The immortal in God has a correspondence in man which is also indestructible. In the growing of wheat, the chaff at a certain stage of development is useful and indispensable; but the time comes when it has served its purpose, and then it is burned or blown away. The evolutionary process of the unfoldment of the spiritual self begins with a physical basis which is good, in its time and place. The material body in its normal, subordinate position is not evil, but, on the contrary, is useful and expressive on its own plane. But when it mounts the throne and claims to be the ego, it invites destruction; for it is death, and death must be destroyed. If one is trying to identify himself with his spiritual ego and has not yet brought the lower self into subjection, he will not fear the "consuming fire," for only by it can he leave behind those things which are combustible. The burning, to him, will not be burning, for looking beneath the surface he will see that its mission is beneficent. The lurid flame of Love will appall the "old man," for to his distorted vision it will reduce him to ashes; but, like pure gold tried by fire, the divine man will behold God in the furnace with him. The stronger the false claimant clings to his seeming life, the deeper the flame will penetrate. It burns him because it is his true friend. When in a paroxysm of terror in the desperation of the life-and-death contest he feels his life ebbing away, he suddenly awakes to the startling revelation that he is saved, "so as by fire." Divine love will not and cannot be baffled. It will threaten and burn until the last vestige of death and corruption shall have been consumed, when the divine unshaken man will be found intact. The blazing flames of Love will spread and burn until they possess and purify every soul, whether that soul be upon the plane of sense or within the confines of *Hades*.

IX. The Unseen Realm.

THE WORLD is bound in the fetters of the seen. A sensuous and pessimistic cloud darkens and benumbs racial progress and aspiration. Human thought and action are conformed to traditional standards and gauged by external models and maxims.

Life, which is intangible and invisible, expresses itself through organisms, though it is not the result but the cause of organization. All the potency of the universe is resident in spirit, which through orderly energy builds up symmetrical forms. The things around us that seem so solid and enduring are thin shadows cast by that subtle spiritual energy which forms their only basis. The earth itself is one grand cemetery, made up of disintegrated forms, while the great current of life which formerly vitalized them still flows on unspent and undiminished. That which at present is in manifestation, and which our eyes behold, is but an infinitesimal part of the grand Whole. Where is the dust that has not some time been moulded and fashioned by living energy, and that in different shapes repeated,—

> "All that tread
> The globe are but a handful to the tribes
> That slumber in its bosom"?

Says Paul in his Epistle to the Corinthians, "While we look not at the things which are seen, but at the things which are not seen: for the things which are seen are temporal; but the things which are not seen are eternal."

All physical organisms are built *by* their invisible residents and not *for* them. Materialistic science, after much assumption and persistent experiment, has been forced to utterly abandon the theory of spontaneous generation, the attempt to evolve life out of dead or inorganic matter. The doctrine of Biogenesis, which teaches that life originates only in previous life, is abundantly established. Still further, every kind and quality of life organizes itself in that special form of embodiment which exactly corresponds to its nature. The form of a tiger, in every detail, perfectly expresses the tiger life and disposition, and that of a lamb is fashioned by its lamb-like characteristics. Life—animal, human, or divine— is ever carving its own animated statues, and through immutable law sets them up with perfect correspondence and adaptability. The human mind rears its own noble form, moulded and polished in every feature by the unconscious constructive thought and specification of its resident architect. Its outline, vigor, and utility are developed or impaired by the favoring or disfavoring mental states of its owner. The general recognition of the fact that all primary causation is mental or spiritual, would be of untold value to humanity; but even the church has been so materialistic that it has mistakenly located an important part of the causal realm in matter. Physical philosophy has thereby logically concluded that molecular changes in the gray matter of the brain were the *causes* of variations in mental conditions; a remarkable instance of the confusing of cause and effect. Immortal mind subservient to the change of position of a few particles of dust! The same materialistic logic causes men to search in the clay of their bodies for the *cause* of physical or mental ills. Life cannot be reenforced by any mere manipulation of the dust, which is only its outermost circumference and shadow. A changed expression comes from a changed expresser. In order to move a shadow we must change the position of the object which casts it.

Materialism is the bane of humanity. Its malaria has subtly enveloped philosophy, science, theology, therapeutics, religion, creeds, and ethics. Its sordid, hypnotic dream is the fatal spell which holds the world in thraldom. Its great current of selfishness, avarice, pride, and conventionalism sweeps the multitude along by an irresistible momentum. *Pseudo*-science avers that mind is only an attenuated and highly developed form of matter, nothing more, and thus leaves men "without God and without hope in the world." Pessimistic fiction joins hands with it, and lends the artistic skill and charm of its creators to echo its cold mechanical conclusions, and thus enlists the imagination in its unholy warfare. The living, pulsating cosmos becomes a dumb mechanism,—a dead, blank, fatalistic negation.

But turning to a truly scientific interpretation of phenomena, we find that color, form, solidity, extension, and other so-called properties of matter are, in their essence, sensuous limitations. Some years since it was announced with a flourish of trumpets by an eminent materialistic scientist, that all potency was contained in matter, but a correct statement would locate it in mind. Mind is the potter, and matter the clay. The seen world is only a sensuous veil covering unseen reality. The visible is a painted canvas which represents the landscape, but the invisible is the living scenery itself.

A proper discrimination will divide the unseen into two distinct economies,—one in a sense material, though invisible, and another which is purely spiritual. The first may be said to include force, attraction, cohesion, electrical and chemical energy, the inter-planetary ether, and perhaps other imponderable agents. The higher realm of pure spirit includes the One Infinite Mind and its individualized, human expressions and their attributes. Immutable law provides that all energy and expressiveness have their rise in causal planes which are higher than those of their phenomena, and we infer that all primary causation is located in the realm of spirit. The next lower, or the invisible material world, is the residence of secondary causes, and forms a connecting and intermediary link; and still below is the seen, which is the crude and entirely passive ultimate. Is there a corresponding chain of sequence in the individual economy? Does the ego telegraph its commands to the various bodily members by means of electrical energy? Such is the accepted doctrine of able scholars.

It is not within the scope of this work to philosophize regarding the intermediary realm, for that technically lies within the boundaries of physical science. Some of the researches in this department however are of intense interest. Among the deductions of modern investigation, it is claimed that what we call matter is in reality only "points of force;" that the atoms of which bodies are composed never touch each other, and that the inter-planetary space which was formerly supposed to be a mere vacuum is filled with an ether more dense than steel. The "rhythmic hypothesis" leads to the supposition that various systems, economies, and civilizations may exist together, be amidst and pass through each other, without either being aware of the proximity of the other.

Are the spiritual bodies of our friends and neighbors—yea, and of the race—who have passed on, all about and among us continually? Such a conclusion seems probable from analogy, science, revelation, and intuition.

"Millions of spiritual creatures walk the earth
Unseen, both when we wake and when we sleep."

It is far more reasonable to believe that on the Mount of Transfiguration, Moses and Elias were disclosed to the sharpened spiritual perception of the disciples, than that they came from a far-away paradise. When Elisha prayed that his servant's eyes might be opened, "he saw: and, behold, the mountain was full of horses and chariots of fire round about Elisha." They were already there, but the vision was conditioned upon the spiritual perception of the young man.

Our notional materialism confers substantiality upon gold, silver, iron, houses, lands, railroads; but as they are not real forces, we are guilty of unconscious idolatry. They are nothing until acted upon by the unseen; but a thought-wave, idea, or doctrine can transform nations.

We are constantly misled by identifying ourselves with our sensuous nature. Men carelessly, and even jocosely, speak of those who have passed on, as ghosts, shades, phantoms, spectres, and apparitions. But much more exactly such definitions would fit the visible body, which with scientific exactness may be called an unsubstantial appearance. Men say, we do not want abstractions; give us *terra firma*. Yet but for the subtle force of the unseen, the earth itself would disintegrate and dissolve into mere vapor.

The universal cosmos is an expression of divine thought and energy from within, not from the exterior. Every human creation is mentally produced before it takes on material form. A locomotive is the thought of an expert mechanic embodied in iron, steel, and brass. Nature is a living, pulsating, divine energy, expressed to us upon a plane which is fitted to our sentient perception. We can follow back lines of causation, step by step, until we are overwhelmed with a sense of the Great Primal Energy—God—who is the basis of all things. This ultimate, when translated to us, is Love, which we may regard as the one universal principle, on the plane of the spiritual universe, corresponding to gravitation in the intermediate realm.

The human soul contains an unseen universe within itself. Man is a microcosm, though the statement has been regarded by many as poetic rather than scientific. It is also exact to affirm that he can cognize nothing objective except its counterpart and correspondence exist within him. If one, through conformity to law, regulate his universe within, so as to bring it into harmonious relations with the universe without, he is in at-one-ment with the divine order. In the macrocosm the spiritual realm is dominant and supreme. If the microcosm be otherwise, because of the dominance of the seen, it becomes discordant and chaotic. Every soul-universe is gradually taking such color and quality as will perfectly manifest its inmost consciousness.

In the spiritual domain there are various spheres of attainment which the Christ denominated as "many mansions." The divine forces of involution which have eternally radiated from God are gathered, individualized, and evolved into increasingly compact forms in their upward return towards the Father's House. Divine involution is the basis and inspiration of human evolution. If the life principle had not first been involved into the acorn, it could not be evolved into the oak. The potential "sons of God" have been upon a journey into a far country, but their inherent heritage only becomes manifest during their return towards the Paternal Mansion. To human sense the upward course is a narrow, thorny path, but to spiritual discernment it is the King's highway.

Said Edwin Arnold, "Where does nature show signs of breaking off her magic, that she should stop at the five senses, and the sixty or seventy elements? Nothing but ignorance and despondency forbids that the senses, so etherialized and enhanced, and so fitly adapted to fine combinations of an advanced entity, would discover art divinely elevated, science splendidly expanding, bygone loves and sympathies explaining and obtaining their purpose, activities set free for vaster cosmic service, abandoned hopes and efforts realized in rich harvests at last, regrets and repentances softened by the discovery that although in this universe nothing can be forgiven, everything may be repaid and repaired. To call such a life Heaven, or the Hereafter, is a temporary concession to the illusions of speech and thought. It would rather be a state, a plane of faculties, to expand again into other and higher states or planes; the slowest and lowest in the race of life coming in last, but each, everywhere finally attaining."

Man is not hedged in, for he has God-like prerogatives, and his spiritual native heath is within the limits of the divine nature. The whole unbounded universe is his, subject only to the developed capacity of his own openness to receive his inheritance. The declaration of Paul that, "all things are yours," though positive, has been given little significance.

Space, time, locality, and other sensuous phenomena are but provisional forms of thought. The soul during its long process of spiritual evolution utilizes for a short time its bodily instrument as a disciplinary and educational agency. But, by homage to the form instead of the substance, man has bound himself by unnumbered limitations, and turned his back upon his princely heritage. He has loaded the simple and natural Christ-religion with superficial traditions, and is struggling under dead weights, which he has placed upon his own shoulders.

If we would listen intently we might hear the divine voice within assuring us that God is our life; that spirit is the only substantial entity, and that love is the only law.

In order to build our microcosm of divine and enduring substance, we must invoke a mental environment of the real, the good, and the lovely; for thought is constantly furnishing our building material and placing it in the structure. The most ideal of all attainments is the development of the power to "see God." We first learn to behold Him in Nature, which reveals Him as Creator and Father. By the next step we are able to behold the divine image in humanity around us, which is the degree of the Son, or incarnation. The third and highest attainment is God dwelling in our own consciousness through a recognized oneness, and this may be denominated the degree of the Spirit. These form a trinity of recognition, or three aspects of the Eternal One. Everything in and around us thus becomes a living revelation of God.

In conceiving of the spiritual world we are too much inclined to identify it with a future life. It is there, but also here. It is that rich, divine realm in which our souls live, move, and nourish themselves, both here and hereafter. It is the outflow of the superabundant life and love of God upon which we feed and grow. All nature is an object-lesson showing the wisdom and beneficence which pulsate in the invisible counterpart behind it. Our spiritual vision must be sharpened so that we can penetrate through forms and veils and behold the warm exuberance beneath. The spiritual faculty within is always in touch with God, and is the organ through which we commune with spiritual spheres. The intellect may reason *about* God, but only the intuitive perception can see and feel Him.

We may not suppose that of necessity one gets deeper into the spirit-world by the act of laying off the material organism. There is an outer and an inner, a spiritual and unspiritual, there, as well as here. True spirituality on either plane is only gained by earnest aspiration. It is often thought that when the body, with its clogs and limitations, is laid off, great spiritual progress can be made at a bound; but orderly development can only be gradual in any condition. Form, locality, climate, and plane have little to do with soul-progress, which is only made by a growing illumination in its divine centre. Life, love, and truth must be earnestly sought for their own intrinsic sakes. The earthly, selfish, and grovelling thought-currents must be checked and overcome hereafter as well as in the present embodiment. Sinful and debasing mental states will still build up structures of their own correspondences, and only by slow and difficult processes will they be demolished or transformed. The base will attract the base to them, each after their own kind and quality. Men, there as here, will dwell in their own evil natures, pursuits, loves, and companionships until the discord becomes insufferable, and the burning hunger can no longer be satisfied with husks; then amidst self-inflicted suffering they will turn and climb the toilsome ascent back toward the ever-open Father's House.

The present is the time to "walk in the spirit." "Behold, now is the acceptable time; behold, now is the day of salvation." The external life is changeful and tumultuous because the internal, divine life is not yet unfolded. A spiritual glow at the soul-centre sends its invigorating energy outward into ultimates, and thereby corrects and clarifies the domain of illusions, shadows, and disorders. Harmony can be found only in the unseen.

The real universe to each one is that which is built of thoughts, mental states, and imaginations. No evil can ever harm us except as we build it into our world with our own hands.

Let us ascend the mount of spiritual vision, and with intuitive eye glance at the broad outlook. Upon one hand we behold a glorious landscape, made up of the fertile meadows of living, spiritual consciousness; masses of color composed of the flowers of brotherly love; shady groves, where every tree is an elevating thought; the luxuriant foliage of good works, mountains of pure spiritual aspiration, crystal streams of altruism, all lying upon the shore of the great, shimmering, boundless sea of divine and human oneness. We may roam in these meadows, bask in this sunlight, gather these flowers, drink of these fountains, and revel in this scenery. Our divine heritage confers upon us creative energy, and such a domain is of our own invoking and uprearing.

But, on the other hand, our moral freedom makes it possible for us to erect—even ignorantly or carelessly—a negative world, unseen, but subjectively real. Shall we glance at it? Pestilential morasses exhale the miasma of selfishness; the gnarled trunks of its slimy trees are twisted and bent with envy and sensuality; its mountains are volcanoes, out of whose fiery deeps are belched forth showers of evil imaginings, burning passions, and appetites; its turbid streams are stagnant and clogged with avarice and ambition, and its very atmosphere is clammy with materialism and fetichism. The wolves of malignant thought prowl within its desolate shades, and the serpents of cunning deceit and earthy instinct disport themselves in its damp recesses. Are we unconsciously building a habitation in such a subjective universe? When the present dream of sense is ended and we leave the material plane, our *thought* world will be our *real* world. As a mason sets brick after brick in a growing structure, so we are building thoughts and mental states into our unseen abodes. Only as divine and unchanging material is built into the house that we are constructing will it be able to endure the floods and tempests which are impending.

If man's ego or personality has not been wrought into the enduring part of his being, how much remains of him when he leaves the mortal form behind? Every idol, whether wealth, ambition, sensuality, and even the lower selfhood, will be stripped away, and how then will the soul recognize itself? Only that will remain which cannot be "shaken." The lower spheres of the unseen world retain the essence of earthiness and mortality. Men will continue to chase unreal phantoms and to embrace shadows, until a starving condition of their lean souls will constrain them to turn and seek that which is real.

Does animalized individuality possess a surviving personal consciousness, or must the life-force—which in its essence cannot be destroyed—be turned back to make another trial in some other form or condition?

In the disintegration of the dogma of an arbitrary hell imposed from without, we must beware of minimizing the peril of one which is self-made, that will burn out the dross as unsparingly as it is separated in a refiner's crucible. So far as we identify the ego with the body and the "carnal mind," we shall be lost, and that by law, immutable, and even beneficent.

A character religion is far more searching in its test of foundations than is a religion of dogma. It penetrates to the thoughts and intents of the heart. It goes beneath externals, and deals directly with the inmost springs of being. If one is taught that salvation is based upon righteousness which is outside of himself, he is not inclined to use much care in the examination of his own superstructure. In no degree can ordinances, creeds, and sacraments fill the place of spiritual attainment.

We may dwell beneath the visible seething surface of things, and thus link the ego to the unchangeable. The unseen, the ideal, and the spiritual will then stand out in high relief in our consciousness, until we are moulded by them. The whole invisible realm in and around us is surcharged with spiritual potency and life. If we open the portals of our being, it will flow in and inspire and invigorate.

"When one that holds communion with the skies
  Has fill'd his urn where these pure waters rise,
  And once more mingles with us meaner things,

'Tis e'en as if an angel shook his wings."

We are living in an eternal fountain of strength, and yet are weak; we are encompassed with good, and yet behold evil; health is in infinite supply, and still we groan with pain and disease; order and symmetry are ours, but we are filled with discord and confusion: and all because we abide in the seen and transitory.

The exact nature of the future unseen universe has not been disclosed. Can Revelation and spiritual discernment give a faint hint of its glories? Paul declares that, "Eye hath not seen nor ear heard, neither have entered into the heart of man the things which God hath prepared for them that love him." Saint John "the divine," in the Apocalypse, by means of symbolic imagery paints a picture of its splendors limited only by the power of human language.

Can we, through the telescope of spirit, catch a glimpse of a pure soul, who after a quick and unconscious transition lands upon the delectable shore? A new but real universe is unveiled. Gathered to welcome the new initiate are the dear friends and neighbors who already are citizens. Hands are clasped, and a warm unison of love thrills through reunited souls. Everything which has been lost is found. Parents fold long-absent children in fond embrace, and brothers, sisters, and dear ones are restored and welcomed. The newly arrived celestial candidate is taken by the hand and introduced to grand spiritual activities, and his willing powers enlisted in unexpected and delightful ministries of loving service. Amazing opportunities for spiritual advancement open before him. What wonderful visions! What restoration and compensation! What a succession of far-reaching vistas! How many mysteries explained and questionings satisfied! What a blossoming of new beauty, color, and fragrance, of which he has been all unaware! How many new spiritual senses unfolded! What journeys of exploration, untrammelled by the limitations of time and space! What an expansion of knowledge! What a golden sunshine of love revealed to the enraptured gaze as rapidly as its brightness can be endured! What grand missionary tours to planes below to carry help, guidance, and instruction! What illimitable cycles of spiritual progression stretch out and wind upward towards the Great White Throne!

X. Evolution as a Key.

THE EVOLUTIONARY philosophy of progress is well established. Like many other phases of truth, it has come into recognition gradually, having to overcome much misconception and opposition. In the long course of the human evolution of truth, there comes, in its own time and place, the perception of the law of evolution itself. Until recently it has generally been regarded as unfriendly to religion, contrary to revelation, and as closely allied to materialism. Its unwilling reception by theological systems is an added example of the oft-repeated alarms which the Church has felt when confronted with unexpected scientific discoveries and advances. Religion—so called—has been so artificial, external, and unnatural, that it has been constantly apprehensive lest some new development would discredit or undermine its authority. It has been admitted that in the "natural" realm, truth could not antagonize other truth; but religion, having been placed upon a supernatural basis, has instinctively been suspicious of new light and investigation. But it is becoming evident that evolution and all well-founded science are not only friendly but absolutely confirmatory of whatever is vital and inherent in true religion.

That which has been called religion, and that which has been denominated science, for centuries have faced each other in an antagonistic attitude, each dealing such blows as could possibly be inflicted upon a supposed enemy. The nearest approach to a compromise which was practicable consisted of a tacit understanding that each was utterly distinct from its opponent, and occupied a realm separated from it by a well-defined boundary line. Upon this ground an armistice was possible on the basis of mutual non-interference. Science claimed to be "natural;" but by this term she really meant materialistic, while religion gloried in being "supernatural," which, translated, signified unnatural. For centuries past science has made continuous sallies and advances, while religion—as a dogmatic system—has correspondingly retreated. Stronghold after stronghold has fallen, until, to superficial observers, it looks almost as if the final storming of the last religious citadel was at hand.

But these centuries of conflict have been only a long, false, feverish dream. We awake, rub our eyes, and find that in reality science, religion, and evolution are not only friendly, but are sisters of one family. They are bound by the strongest ties of consanguinity, and each finds its fulness and completion in the others. The past differences have been wholly due to masks that were put on, and held on, by human prejudice. The dream is ended, the masks removed, and a grand family reconciliation and reunion is taking place.

It is manifestly impracticable, within the limits of this chapter, to attempt any general exposition of so great a philosophy as that of evolution. A brief outline of significant points indicative of its utility in explaining and enforcing the principles of vital, spiritual religion is all that is proposed.

The term evolution is defined as "the act of unrolling or unfolding;" "the process of growth and development." In the province of biology it is the name of the progression or successive steps by which any living organism, vegetable or animal, advances to more perfect and determinate conditions. In its widest sense it comprises the development and improvement,—in accord with natural law,—not only of organic life, but of all human institutions, religions, theologies, civilizations, ethics, and spirituality. Its universal trend permeates mind and matter, and pervades the entire illimitable cosmos. As an eternal law it involves progress from the lower to the higher; from the simpler to the more complex; from the less perfect to the more perfect; from the indeterminate to the determinate.

"Time's noblest offspring is the last."

Evolution explains and shows the links and relations between innumerable facts that otherwise are disconnected and unintelligible. Like all other natural laws its philosophy is indispensable in a grand economy of harmony and unity.

Perhaps its most noticeable conflict with traditional and dogmatic beliefs is in its theory of creation. The former supposition that the earth was created out of nothing in the space of six days by an act of volition on the part of God, and that the process was then finished, is utterly discredited. Even when the six days have been extended to six ages, or epochs, the difficulty is not removed. Creation was supposed to have been performed by the fiat of a wonder-working Creator, who Himself was outside of all phenomena, by a supernatural—that is, a *not* natural—process. The undeveloped human mind always had a liking for the marvellous and magical, which inclines it toward such a hypothesis, rather than toward the concept of orderly, gradual, and natural development. An eternal unfolding process, while displaying infinite wisdom, order, foresight, and beneficence on the part of God, lacks the dramatic aspect which, though a relic of antique barbarism, has always gratified the human fancy. What a low conception of the Deity to view Him as an omnipotent Magician! How far more ennobling the idea of a Father who is orderly, lawful, and natural! How much higher infinite Reason than infinite Unreason! How much more God-like, a God manifesting Himself through the beauty and harmony of natural progression, than one who operates with the spasmodic vehemence of an infinite Jove!

The opposite extreme is the hypothesis put forth by an earthy materialism. With a vainglorious desire to get along without God in the universe, it unconsciously pays homage to matter as a real power. In an economy of such wonderful adjustment, marvellous perfection, wise foresight, and means exactly adapted to ends, what more irrational than to credit all to blind, unconscious dust? It is only a seeming refinement of the idea to disguise it in the terms of a technical scientific phraseology. No; the grand old cosmos did not grow of itself, nor, on the other hand, did it spring forth at the dramatic waving of a divine wand.

"All nature is but art, unknown to thee;
All chance, direction, which thou canst not see,
All discord, harmony not understood;
All partial evil, universal good;
And spite of pride, in erring reason's spite,
One truth is clear, Whatever is, is right."

Creation is defined as development, or as investing with new form, rather than as making something out of nothing. Astronomical research proves that creation is perpetual, and that there is an endless series of worlds and systems in all stages of development. In speaking of evolution in its relation to the idea of God, Professor Le Conte says, "If the sustentation of the universe by the law of gravitation does not disturb our belief in God as the Sustainer of the universe, there is no reason why the origin of the universe by the law of evolution should disturb our faith in God as the Creator of the universe. It is evident that if evolution be materialism, then is gravitation also materialism; then is every law of Nature and all science materialism."

While there appears to be a steady progression in the ascending scale of life, sentiency, and individuation, a more critical study discloses certain boundary lines or planes, and when each of these is gained there is a new birth, or a sudden assumption of unprecedented powers and more complex organization. When the conditions are fully ripened, an evolutionary step takes place, thus introducing another form, new relations to environment, virtually a new world.

Professor Le Conte, in formulating the ascending scale or series of great steps, makes the following classification: "First, the plane of elements; second, the plane of chemical compounds; third, the plane of vegetal life; fourth, the plane of animal life; and fifth the plane of rational life."

We would add a sixth distinctive plane, that of the spiritual realm in human development. There is a well-defined boundary between this and the rational or intellectual plane next below. When each ascending step is taken, new phenomena appear, not merely excelling the former in degree, but so unlike as to constitute a new creation. Let us briefly review these planes, and note their transitions and distinctions.

The first, or plane of the elements, may be represented as the divine protoplasmic energy, diffused, generalized, unorganized, and in no degree gathered or compacted. Here is resident vitality of marvellous potency, but in an elemental and primal stage.

The plane of chemical compounds is a step higher, and a gain has been made in quality, affinity, and determinateness; but compactness and organization are yet wanting.

The next advance—the plane of vegetal life—seems like a long step, and is characterized by great changes and added powers. Energy has been gathered, organized, and individuated, as shown in a centred, manifested life. New laws of growth and relations to environment have been assumed, and integration and subsequent disintegration of form, but not of life, have been established.

The next step brings us to the plane of animal life. Added to organization and individuation, are locomotion, sensation, will, and instinct. The life-force is clothed in a form which perfectly expresses the peculiar nature of each species or class that is found within the boundaries of this widely comprehensive division.

Advancing to the plane of human, rational life, instinct, as a governing force, is left behind, and reason assumes control. Here is the human intellect with all its multiform powders and capabilities. Here is moral freedom and the conscious power of choice, which, though errant, marks a great advance beyond blind instinct with all its exactitude. In this department, moral and ethical considerations have their place, though they are still colored and swayed by the passions, appetites, and self-seeking, which have been brought over from the animal plane below. The realm of intellect contains a wide complexity and variety, not only retaining more or less animality, but also anticipating somewhat from the spiritual domain above. It furnishes a testing-ground, and even a battle-field, where the forces from above and those from below wage a warfare for supremacy.

The next step leads to the spiritual plane, which is the crowning attainment of humanity. All that is noble and pure of the intellectual plane is preserved; and, while its contribution becomes secondary and subservient, its real beauty and utility are thereby enhanced. The spiritual plane is the seat of the intuitive faculty,—the illuminated soul-centre,—and involves the enthronement of a spiritual, in the place of a material consciousness. It brings into manifestation the divine image, and thereby reveals the intrinsic oneness of God and man. Being the centre of the primary and supreme causation, it shapes material conditions, and inaugurates general wholeness and harmony. It creates its own corresponding environment, and rules and profits by circumstances which are seemingly adverse, instead of being subservient to them.

The religion of creed, dogma, ritual, and ordinance has its seat in the intellectual realm, although in the proportion that it is pure and internal it survives the transition. From the altitude of the spiritual Mount, immortality is not a theory but a known fact. There is a distinct perception that continued existence and unfoldment are not dependent upon the continuance of the material base when it has been outgrown.

In the great everlasting cycle of creation the primal energy which God first *involved* into the lowest, most general, and indeterminate conditions, is, at length, through a series of grand steps, gathered, organized, individuated, and evolved into "sons of God," in which form the return is made to the "Father's House."

Has Christ a place in the evolutionary philosophy? Most assuredly. Yes; and one which is of supreme importance. It follows that humanity should reach its perfect expression and model in the ideal man, who was also the "Son of God," filled with the divine fulness. All men are images of God; but Jesus was the only one in whom the likeness has been perfectly disclosed and manifested. On the intellectual plane perhaps he did not excel all other men, but his divine and human spiritual identity gave him a supreme altitude. The ideal of each plane lies not only in its own perfect completion, but also in a birth from above. Humanity, in Jesus the Christ, receives an ideal demonstration of its Godhood, which meets it on the spiritual plane. Here man in his upward evolvement towards his goal arrives at that point where he is a sharer and partaker in the Deific nature and prerogatives. The human blossoms into the divine, and thereby perfects its humanity. God comes into man, and supplements and rounds out the crudeness that adhered from former environment.

But it may be urged that the perfect Ideal, by the uniform order of evolution, should not appear until the completion of the spiritual course, rather than near its beginning. Upon this point a significant quotation from Professor Le Conte may profitably be given, as the high rank of his researches is unquestioned. In speaking of the new factor on the highest evolutionary plane, he says, "This factor is *the conscious voluntary co-operation of the human spirit in the work of its own evolution. The method of this new factor consists essentially in the formation, and especially in the voluntary pursuit, of ideals.* In organic evolution species are transformed by the *environment.* In human evolution *character* is transformed by *its own ideal.* Organic evolution is by *necessary* law; human evolution is by voluntary effort, i.e., by *free* law. Organic evolution is, *pushed* onward and upward from behind and below; human evolution is *drawn* upward and forward from above and in front by the attractive force of ideals. Thus the ideal of organic evolution cannot appear until the end; while the attractive ideals of human evolution *must* come, whether only in the imagination or realized in the flesh, but must come somehow *in the course*. The most powerfully attractive ideal ever presented to the human mind, and therefore the most potent agent in the evolution of human character, is *the Christ*. This ideal must come, whether in the imagination or in the flesh I say not, but must come somehow *in the course*, and not at the end. At the end the whole human race, drawn upward by this ideal, must reach the fulness of the stature of the Christ." And again, "At a certain stage we catch glimpses of the *absolute* moral ideal. Then our gaze becomes fixed, and we are thenceforward drawn upward forever. The human race has already reached a point when the absolute ideal of character is attractive. This Divine ideal can never again be lost to humanity."

The Christ is like a great magnet in his drawing power, and thereby quickens the evolution of ideal character. As the attractive force of the earthy wanes in human consciousness, men co-operate with the lifting power from above, not only by their own personal aspirations, but by active effort in aiding those around them.

Does the evolutionary key unlock any of the mysteries of what is theologically known as the "Fall of Man"? With all becoming humility, let us attempt its application. We may think of Adam and Eve, not as the names of a single human pair, but as the types used to designate that transitional step when the race crossed the boundary line which lies between Instinct and Reason. Pre-Adamic man was an animal. Like other animals he was not ashamed of his nakedness, and in common with his kingdom was governed by brutish instincts and appetites. He made his habitation in dens and caves of the earth, and possessed only those faint foreshadowings of reason that we now behold in the highest animal intelligence. Instinct, though blind, is exact. The bee forms the honey-cell with perfect geometrical proportion, and the web of the spider is a marvel of regularity and perfection. The bird makes no mistake in singing its song nor in building its nest, and the beaver no error in the construction of his dam. Instinct is a wonderful combination of crudeness and perfection. It makes neither mistakes nor improvements. The all-pervading divine energy resident in the animal shines through, reflecting its perfection and uniformity, though in actual expression it is limited and cannot rise higher than its crude medium. The song of the bird is God singing through the bird, for the melody is only an overflowing of one of the multiform channels of the divine exuberance shaped by the unreasoning instrument through which it passes. Instinct, we may then interpret as the primal or Deific profusion shining through a medium which is involuntary and unreasoning, with an unchanging level of attainment. Bearing this concept of animal instinct in mind, what is the significance of the "Fall"? It was a passage from irresponsibility to responsibility, from innocence to possible guilt, from blind animal passivity to the knowledge and choice of good or evil. In reality the transition from instinct to reason was a *rise*—a grand evolutionary step upward. However, the quick mistakes of inexperienced reason, as contrasted with the uniform exactness of former instinct, made it appear like a veritable fall. To human consciousness it *was* a fall, and it was natural that tradition so declared it. Mistaken and stumbling reason, though so full of seeming disaster when compared with perfect instinct, was only a delusive fall, for it was—up-hill. Reason, with all its misconceptions and errancy, is far above instinct, because it contains the elements of voluntary choice, gradual improvement, and, in due time, character. If one who has the inherent ability to climb a hill stumbles and finds himself at its foot, he is yet, in a true sense, higher than one who is farther up, but who is incapable either of stumbling or climbing. Thus, the theological dogma of "the Fall," which through the ages has been such a difficult problem, when interpreted in the light of the evolutionary economy is thoroughly solved and made intelligible.

Within the boundaries of *human* evolution, the three great planes or stages of progress may be classed as instinct, reason, and intuition, or as animality, intellectuality, and spirituality. This is the only order in which they can come, and sooner or later every member of the human family must pass over the King's highway which runs through them. While a great majority of the race is now upon the intellectual plane, there has been brought forward a great residuum of animality, but without that exact instinct which was formerly a saving element. The gleams from the spiritual plane, which shoot backwards as well as forwards, modify and partially illuminate the intellectual domain, and impart to it an increasing inspiration.

The intuitional realm brings again to light the precision of instinct, and glorifies it with the highest exercise of reason, and then transforms it with its own divine exaltation. It is here that the Father's likeness is unveiled, and man touches and becomes one with God. The perfect accuracy of instinct is revived in intuition, but it is infinitely elevated by the illumination of intelligence and freedom. Animality, before intellectuality is reached, is ignorant, involuntary innocence; but spirituality is voluntary, achieved character. Virtue gains all its solid fibre and quality through the process of overcoming.

"Great truths are dearly bought. The common truth,
  Such as men give and take from day to day,
  Comes in the common walk of easy life,
  Blown by the careless wind across our way.

Great truths are greatly won, not found by chance,
  Nor wafted on the breath of summer dream,
  But grasped in the great struggle of the soul,
  Hard buffeted with adverse wind and stream.

Wrung from the spirit in hard hours

Of weakness, solitude, perchance of pain;
Truth springs like harvest from the well-ploughed field,
And the soul feels it has not wept in vain."

The plane of spirituality is not fully attained until a decisive victory is gained over lower conditions. Those conditions, when normal, have their legitimate place, but the time comes when they must be outgrown. To linger in lower forms when the soul is ready for a higher moulding, is to arrest development and violate the divine order. Any turning back, or even standing still, involves penalty and decay. The trend of the universal economy must be observed, otherwise friction and disaster follow. The law of progress is one and the same for the individual, the race, and the whole universe of God.

The great distinguishing feature of animality is selfishness, while that of the spiritual plane is unselfishness. These states are as opposite as the poles, and the entire length of the ladder of human evolution stretches out between them.

The problem of the existence of evil and its relation to evolutionary law having been touched upon in a former chapter (The Universality of Law), need not be taken up in this connection. The evolutionary philosophy classifies things as higher and lower, rather than as good and evil. The lower is the soil in which the higher takes root. By this growth the higher gains a breadth and grandeur which could only come from adverse conditions outgrown and left behind.

Science, evolution, and true religion interpret, indorse, and supplement each other, and are all indispensable in forming the great sphere of Truth. Each must contribute its part to produce a grand diapason of harmony.

Evolution is the long-sought clew that has been needed to unify and interpret all phenomena. Through its aid, discordant and misplaced theories, philosophies, and institutions find their true place, and are brought into accord. It translates all history, and brings orderly progression out

XI. From the Old to the New.

"In the attrition of theological thought, the harvests of centuries are ground up, and in the winds of discussion a good deal of chaff is blown away. But the elements of the bread of life still remain, and the world was never more hungry for it than to-day."

WHITHER ARE we drifting? There is an irresistible movement in the realm of religious thought which any careful estimate will show to be of remarkable magnitude. Many are anxiously watching the drift, and some are apprehensive as to the security of what they feel to be foundation principles. Are there substantial verities? and, if so, how shall we distinguish their solid outlines from those temporary forms which are liable to dissolve while we gaze upon them?

There is a growing conviction that the organized church, by slow degrees, is losing its hold upon the community, and that its influence, as a force to mould society, is waning. The utterances of the pulpit are becoming less authoritative in their tone, and less weighty in their impressiveness upon human thought and conduct. The Bible is receiving such exhaustive criticism and analysis as formerly would have been deemed sacrilegious. The tribute paid to creeds, dogmas, and ceremonial religion, is lessening; and the reverence which environed scholastic theology in human consciousness is slowly fading. Faith in the importance and efficacy of external symbols, ordinances, and rituals, is perceptibly weakening, and ecclesiastical assumptions are being re-examined.

That there is such a general tendency will hardly be questioned, either by those who regard it as salutary, or by others who believe it to be fraught with disaster. Is the world drifting into materialism, and are the spiritual and divine elements in human character losing their power? or is it only a fusing and recasting of old forms to meet the burning conditions and necessities of the present age? Watchman! what of the night? Do the unrest and confusion presage the dawn of a brighter day?

To determine the significance of the transition, the divergence must be noted between the formulated thought of the past and the actual thought of to-day, which, as a rule, is yet unexpressed in formal statements. The distance already traversed from the decaying but still authoritative ancient creeds varies materially, even among the subdivisions of that great composite body known as the Protestant Church. The influence of the drift in permeating the Roman system is less pronounced, because its unified organization and traditional conservatism render it more impervious to progressive influences. As the tendency of advanced thought is most noticeable in what are known as the Evangelical branches of the Protestant Church, the transition, as seen among them, will mainly be considered.

The letter of formulated theological standards, with few trifling exceptions, has not been modified so as to correspond with actual present belief. The great creeds of Christendom include the Nicene of the fourth century, the Apostles' and the Athanasian which were formulated a little later, and that which is known as the Westminster Confession of the seventeenth Century. Some less important doctrinal statements have obtained limited acceptance, but the basis for them is generally found in one or all of these great systems. Here and there some minor organizations have rounded the angles: but, generally speaking, nineteenth-century theological thought has no authoritative form except such as was cast by councils which gathered from of spasmodic confusion. It solves problems in biology and anthropology, and explains and anticipates progression in governmental systems, morals, sociology, and religion. It has to do with spirit as well as matter; divinity as well as humanity. It silences all pessimistic philosophy; and high upon the folds of its irresistible banner is inscribed the watchword—Excelsior. However good and perfect the to-day, it bids men look for a better to-morrow.

The misconstructions of biblical interpretation are removed when the Bible is approached as an evolutionary, sacred literature. Regeneration, which was regarded as supernatural, is seen as a natural step in progressive unfoldment.

The persistence of the substratum of animalism in mankind is shown by the outcroppings of war, strife, envy, and division, which continually come to the surface of human history. The murky clouds of pessimism and egotism are also exhalations from the same unwholesome plane.

Evolution is progression in life and not in matter. All the great steps are different qualities of attained internal character. Matter never progresses; which proves that it is only a form of expression. The identical physical material appears and re-appears in higher and lower forms of life, therefore it has no character of its own. The atoms which form the body of a saint are the same that have made up the body of a plant or animal. The progression is in the immaterial *reality*. It is important that this great distinction be preserved, for thereby the sophistry of materialism is exposed. Evolution is the progression of ascending inherent *qualities* of life; and these incidentally make use of sensuous and temporary translations. Every kind of *life* grows, but shapes of outward manifestation disintegrate.

For the individual and the race, life is becoming broader, richer, diviner; and this law of progress is eternal.

The divine order cannot be fragmentary or broken off, and therefore progressive unfoldment will continue in the future state as here. Time and space being ephemeral can interpose no resistance to the eternal sweep of this great Law, which finds its sublimest field for exercise in the human soul.

Human unfoldment is pressing on towards the supreme ideal of racial love and harmony. The heavenly condition becomes increasingly distinct and complete as the great evolutionary highway is traversed. That love which now flows in a few narrow personal channels will broaden to take in all humanity, and its concentric circles will bring God and all His children together in loving unity.

two to sixteen centuries ago. The great conservative Presbyterian Church of the United States has felt enough of the "ground swell" to cause it to begin the task of revising its Westminster Confession, which, until recently, was regarded as too sacred to be questioned. Its revision committee, however, has been instructed against any change which would in any degree impair the "Calvinistic system." Time will determine whether or not the tidal wave can be stayed at that point.

While knowledge in every other department is expanding so constantly that new text-books replace old ones in rapid succession, is it possible that during centuries the loftiest of subjects has received no new illumination? Truth indeed is unchangeable; but the human apprehension of it is ever growing and brightening.

The great drift has opposite meanings to those who view it from different standpoints. There are those who cling tenaciously to the Old because it is old, and others who reach anxiously forward to the New because they see in it progress and higher development. The ultra-conservatives are confused by the movement; and to them it is only loss, because they are not plastic to new light and revelation. To their anxious gaze the drift is from a sound theology towards an uncertain and unsound theology; from an authoritative Bible towards a rationalistic Bible; from a solid, compact, religious system towards a negative and sentimental one. Not delving beneath the troubled surface of the drift, they behold an obtrusive materialism and scepticism, but fail to recognize these as the logical and natural reaction from their own past strained institutionalism. The new theology looks to them like a limp, boneless body, destitute of form and authority, but yet as persistently iconoclastic in its temper.

To the perverted vision of the atheist and materialist, the drift has the appearance of Hearing their own position. Having for so long looked upon ceremony and dogmatism as *constituting* religion, the decadence of the former seems like the ending of the latter. Color-blindness to spiritual forces incapacitates them to interpret the mystery of a hidden and higher life. All the shafts they have hurled would have fallen harmless had they been aimed at religion itself, instead of at its externalities, excrescences, and shams. The materialist is utterly unable to cognize the spiritual life, because he is familiar with no plane higher than that of the intellect.

The religion of external and conflicting systems, ecclesiastical assumption, and sectarian loyalty, is giving place to that which is a renewing and vital force in character; a power to lift mankind out of selfishness and animalism into divine sonship. It is only by such Fruits that it shows its harmonious and heavenly proportions. The tremendous significance of the great transition can hardly yet be estimated, but it is safe to assume that nothing intrinsic can be moved. All truth is anchored to the throne of God, and it will forever remain unshaken. Only the external, the temporary, and the unreal are being sloughed off. All that bears the divine monogram will stand out in bolder relief than ever before. Man is finding his way nearer to God. He is feeling the warm glow of divine oneness within, and no longer uses a telescope in a search for the Father.

A radical divergence between the Old and the New is seen in unlike conceptions regarding the seat of authority in religion. The emphasis of the former is upon that which is external to man, while the latter finds the law of God written in man's own nature. In the primitive church, before ecclesiastical and political policy dominated, the seat of authority was clearly the Spirit— the illuminating internal witness and "Teacher." Says Paul in his First Epistle to the Corinthians, "But he that is spiritual judgeth all things, and he himself is judged of no man." Spiritual perception comprises the only "inerrancy." As that was displaced in the early church by the scholastic and controverted formulas of schools and councils, they usurped the original and divinely constituted source of authority. The church lost its spiritual freedom, and the influx of divine life and love was obstructed. That which men were at liberty to believe was set forth and enacted by the capricious vote of great councils; and by the same method the canon of the Scriptures was selected from the accumulated mass of sacred Hebrew literature. The voice of God in the human soul was drowned by the discordant chorus of theological "hair-splitting" logic and intellectual sophistication. From the second century down to the nineteenth the Christian Church, as a rule, both Roman and Protestant, has yielded homage to human dictation in the shape of external and ecclesiastical "rules" of faith.

The Roman hierarchy, with the Pope at its head, constituted the supreme and unquestioned authority in Christendom down to the Reformation, and still so continues to its millions of real and nominal adherents. Spiritual and political authority early became mingled, with the necessary result that the former was degraded, and brought down to the level of the latter. Following the Reformation, among the Protestants the Bible—or rather that interpretation of it contained in the creeds—was installed as authority in the place of the Pope. When the separation took place, the Papists continued to have an infallible Pope, and the Protestants found it necessary to proclaim an infallible Book. But it was thought necessary to furnish the Book with props, stays, and bandages, as though it could not be trusted to interpret itself. Its proper agency as a mirror and educator—as "profitable for teaching, for reproof, for correction, for instruction, which is in righteousness"—was displaced; and it was made an oracle, whose utterances could only be grasped through external systems which have practically been crowned with authority over the Scriptures themselves.

A fundamental declaration of the creeds is that, "The Bible is the only infallible rule of faith and practice." The Bible nowhere makes such an exclusive claim for itself, but uniformly exalts the Spirit as Guide, Inspirer, Illuminator, and Teacher. If the statement of the creed does not dishonor the Spirit, it is difficult to imagine what declaration could do so more effectually,—"The only rule." If it be the *only* rule, then no other guide exists now, and there was no guide whatever before the Scriptures were collected and canonized. Where did the patriarchs and prophets find their "faith" or determine their "practice"? Was Melchizedek, "King of Righteousness" and "Priest of the Most High God," destitute of *any* rule of "faith"? Is every divine influence which kindles the faith and guides the practice limited to this one "infallible" channel? But to whom is it "infallible"? Not certainly to the scores of different denominations who find unlike doctrines and build up antagonistic creeds from its sacred pages. Is it "infallible" to the Calvinist and the Arminian who each find what is contrary to the other?

Faith is a vital element in life and not a "rule." The creed probably means by faith, that which it is not, a system of doctrine; but numberless systems are founded upon the one Bible. The Scriptures are "profitable" rather than infallible. They are not a revelation, but a record of divine revelations in the souls of men. God is ever in contact with human souls. The one direct and supreme authority is the tribunal of the Spirit in the heart of man's nature. There is the divine image and that is the perfect model. The Bible is of untold utility; but it extols, as above itself, the "teacher which shall guide you into all truth." The loftiest biblical phraseology must receive soul-assimilation before it can be more than ancient history, or external moral experience and theory. If the Bible came down from the skies as an inerrant communication, without any human element or imperfection, it would lose its utility as a reflector and interpreter of human nature and its needs.

Man need not mistake the significance of the Scriptures. If God's voice in the soul be not stifled by external authority, the interpretation of truth will be clear and self-attesting. Practically the Bible can be read in no other way. Touching this point an eminent divine[4] in a recent essay said:—

> "Who is at the reader's elbow, as he reads Exodus and Leviticus, to tell him what is of permanent authority, and what was for the Mosaic dispensation only? Who whispers to us, as we read Genesis and Kings, This is exemplary; this is not? Who sifts for us the speeches of Job, and enables us to treasure as divine truth what he utters in one verse, while we reject the next as Satanic raving? What enables the humblest

---

4. Rev. Marcus Dods, D.D., Professor of New Testament Exegesis in New College, Edinburgh, Scotland.

Christian to come safely through all the cursing Psalms and go straight to forgive his enemy? What tells us we may eat things strangled, though the whole college of Apostles deliberately and expressly prohibited such eating? Who assures us we need not anoint the sick with oil, though James bids us do so? In a word, how is it that the simplest reader can be trusted with the Bible, and can be left to find his own spiritual nourishment in it? Paul solves the whole matter for us in his bold and exhaustive words, 'The spiritual man [the man who has the spirit of Christ] judgeth all things.' This, and this only, is the true touchstone by which all things are tried. Let a man accept Christ and live in his Spirit, and there is no fear that he will reject what Christ means he should receive."

The church "standards" were formulated in an age of great limitations when compared with the present, and remain fixed, while actual belief is constantly changing. The two should agree, but there is an ever-increasing divergence. In many cases the gateway into the church is barred by the required solemn affirmation of dogmas which are practically obsolete. Should dead formulas which are not believed remain inscribed upon its banner? Some say, "Let them stand, but give them new interpretation." But this would be a specious diplomatic stretching and straining of language unworthy even of a secular organization. Positive statements abound, which, while unaccepted, continually receive official and formal assent. The unequivocal dogmas of divinely inflicted endless punishment, election and non-election, preterition, the literal judgment, and the material resurrection, are examples of the untruthfulness of the actual to the theoretical. The Church cannot afford to be more careless and self contradictory—not to say dishonest—than the world. The latter has a contempt for sophistry, and looks upon sincerity as one of the primary elements of religion, in which opinion it is quite correct. The examination of a candidate for ordination, in which a creed must be evaded, and, at the same time solemnly affirmed, is a humiliating spectacle. Religion is a growing, living force. As well thrust an active, vigorous animal into a cast-iron mould as to exactly define all truth in external formula. In either case life is extinguished.

But perversion which retains abandoned statements because human and sectarian pride will not admit past misapprehension, has a subtler degrading influence than is often recognized. It not only forfeits the confidence of the world, but actually darkens Christian character. Hypocrisy is more dangerous than scepticism. Christ never condemned honest doubt, but he did denounce Pharisaism. Sincerity is a gem of the first water, but shams are odious. If one, in the interest of policy, begins a course of plausible concealments and conformities towards a creed that he does not truly accept, his spiritual perception becomes blurred, and moral degeneration sets in. The eye must be single, otherwise darkness follows. A gospel with mental reservations, yea, that is not obviously transparent to the most impartial convictions of truth, is without vitality. The subjective effect of insincerity is decided. One has been taught that certain beliefs are essential to salvation. He finds it impossible to *really* accept them, but dares not make the admission even to himself. He tries to force himself upon external and traditional authority, to believe that which his God-given spiritual perception rejects. He makes believe believe. He stifles the decision of the sacred tribunal of his own soul for the sake of supposed present or future reward. This is immoral because the moral sense is humiliated and degraded. God's law, deeply written in man's constitution, will never condemn him if he honestly seeks truth for its own pure sake. Such an one has a guidance which will never lead him out of the way. That scepticism which is the product of sin or selfishness is not sincere scepticism; but there may be honest doubt about some things which have been called religion, but hardly concerning its vital principles. Whether one be classed as orthodox or heterodox, whether his creed be simple or complex, above all things let him be true to himself, and loyal to his deepest convictions. Any salvation which has no foundation of sincerity and transparency is not salvation at all.

The mission of the gospel is the building of a divine manhood; the purifying and perfecting of life so that robust spirituality may be developed. The human soul is more precious than church or temple, and the inner voice is more infallible than doctrine and dogma. The crucial religious test must be spiritual life and purity, rather than mechanical doctrine, because living, breathing man is of far greater moment than the dry bones of past ages. Individual liberty is sacred. If heresy be honest it will grade higher in the moral scale than sophisticated traditional acceptance. The chanting of the Credo as a spiritual accomplishment must give way to something of the transparent simplicity of the primitive church.

The drift is moving away from the special and supernatural towards the orderly and natural. Nature, in its widest sense, being a translation of God, religion must be natural. Man is the crown and climax of nature, and through it is bound to God. All truth, whether designated as sacred or secular, is divine, and has infinite oneness, relation, and harmony. As well attempt to divide God by hard and sharp lines as to run partitions between related realities. Law, which is unifying and vital, marks out the path along which the divine economy manifests itself.

The old theology was historic and scholastic; but the consensus of present thought emphasizes unselfishness and character. The former was intellectual, the latter intuitional. One was a complicated plan or system outside of man; the other traces the divine outlines within him. The former was argumentative, intolerant, and artificial; the latter, attractive and normal. Human conduct was regulated by the metes and bounds of "Thou shalt not," more than inspired by supreme motive. The old appealed to motives of obligation, duty, and fear, while the ultimate goal of the new is that measure of love which eventually will outlaw the law.

God, from being a jealous, imperious Sovereign, capriciously pleased to select and elect a few of His children, is being exalted by an infinitely higher perception. The human heart warmly responds to the Great Loving Ideal, because the law that love begets love is divinely implanted in man's nature.

The essential Christ is the everlasting manifestation of God's love to man, of which the historic Jesus was an expressive incarnation. The emphasis, from the local and temporary, is being transferred to the unchanging and unseen. Jesus of Nazareth was a divine translation to material man; but the spiritual man, as Paul declared, does not necessarily need to know Christ "after the flesh." His mission was not to placate, purchase, nor to act as a substitute, but to bring abundant life; to interpret divine love, and awaken the already existent divine image.

The Atonement is seen to be an At-one-ment, which on God's part is eternally complete. All the reconciliation is on the part of man. When he practically recognizes God as Love, reconciliation is complete.

The Church is viewed less as an "ark of safety," and more as a means in the development of a higher life. It is useful to just that degree in which it awakens spiritual consciousness, and transforms character into harmony with the divine standard.

The drift is away from a Bible which is an oracle and a fetich, and towards the more honorable concept of a Book which is profitable and progressive. It is the record of glimpses and perceptions which eminent men of old had of God, and of human relations to Him. It is a literature which contains human limitations, but underneath and through them shines the Spirit of Truth. Literalism has dishonored it, and so wrought its letter into external systems that numerous opposing sects all claim the same foundation.

Heaven is changing in human conception from place to ideal spiritual character. It is less a boon, outside of man, gained by purchase, and more a condition of inward oneness with God, reached through pure aspiration and spiritual growth.

Religion is less of a ritual, profession, or accepted creed, and more of an inner unfoldment. Not an unhappy alternative, but a normal human development.

Retribution is no longer vindictive and from without, but an inward condition which we make for ourselves.

The higher life is finding new forms for manifestation, many of which are outside of the boundaries of the organized church. The "Fatherhood of God" and the "brotherhood of man" are brightening in human consciousness. The channels for mutual brotherly aid and sympathy are being deepened, and the links of interdependence are growing stronger. The term neighbor is broadening in significance, and the exuberant overflow of the altruistic spirit is submerging selfish limitations.

The intermingling of divine and human love-currents is becoming more complete by the melting away of man-made barriers. It is axiomatic that man is restless until he finds God, and this he often fails to do because he loses his way among the mazes of scholastic theology. Human systems instead of teaching the divine indwelling have built innumerable by-ways which lead outward. Poets, Mystics, and Quietists, by a more profound insight, have excelled theologians in their interpretations of the divine character. Notwithstanding all the anxiety regarding the great drift, the world is more truly religious to-day than at any time in the past.

The researches of modern science in astronomy, geology, and especially in biology, have greatly broadened recent religious thought. True science is becoming more religious, and religion is seen to be scientific. The traditional theory of the Creation has been obliged to give way to positive evidence that it is continuous and progressive. The grand cycle of progress is found to be a continual involution of primal energy from God, followed by its return in grand, ascending, evolutionary steps. Science is taking in the unseen, as well as the seen universe. Religion, Christianity, and spirituality are as amenable to Law as chemistry and molecules. Man can only be fully interpreted from an evolutionary standpoint. He is a creature of relations. The unit of his history, constitution, development, and destiny is racial in its scope. He cannot be disconnected from his place in the evolutionary scale, for he has vital ties both above and below. The microcosm can only be interpreted by the macrocosm. Evolution is the grand highway which leads to ideals, and ideals are divine standards. When, in the ascending series, man's place is reached, ideals from above become attractive, and he voluntarily co-operates and helps to lift himself; while lower in the scale the pressure is involuntary and from below.

The drift has broadened the domain of biology to a hitherto undreamed-of expansiveness. All life is now recognized as One Principle, differentiated and expressed in an infinite variety of forms and mediums, but still one in essence. God, when considered as Universal Life, is brought into His universe, and into man and all his relations. No new life is created and none destroyed. Life cannot die. Forms perish; but the great universal stream of vitality surges on, unspent and undiminished. Its outward manifestations are kaleidoscopic in swiftness and variety of combination, but there is but One Energy.

In what degree and quality must life be individuated to build up a personal consciousness which will survive the dissolution of its external form? When the form perishes, must not that peculiar personal quality which has identified itself only with outward expression perish also? Physical sensation vanishes, and, so far as that has been counted as the *life*, that life is "lost." All falsities must dissolve, but the real will survive. Only the *true* life, which is on a plane above and independent of the physical *form*, can have conscious personal immortality. None of the lower life-force is lost; but may it not be re-absorbed into the great stream of unconscious energy? It is not the *life*, but the consciousness, that may not endure. That which is linked to an environment must share its destiny. The divine image is man's ideal self. In the degree to which his ego is wrought into this indestructible part of his economy his personality has an immortal basis. When he says, "I," to what does he refer? If to his body, or to his external and sensuous mind, he is in danger of losing what, *to him*, is himself. The external and *that which adheres to it* is subject to disintegration. The ideal in man is immortal, and the ego must be bound to it—yes, *be* it—in order to share its divine permanence. As man links himself to God and Spirit, his ego takes on their eternal attributes. That life, if such there be, which is *essentially* base and external, when the form is dropped will gradually lose its unreal personality. Its unconscious vital force will mingle with the great current of energy which, in due time, will build up *other* forms and *new* personalities, until a *fitness* for survival is finally gained. Thus that familiar aphorism, "The survival of the fittest," when rightly applied, becomes of startling significance.

Religion is a binding to God, and that bond is normal. God-consciousness in the soul of man is the only force which can awaken and uncover the supremest ideal. God has entered human life, and by orderly steps is working out His grand design. The divine exuberance will flow in and fill every vacancy that is made ready in the human soul. Spiritual evolution is continuous, and life is growing richer, sweeter, and broader. Men are joining hands to lift each other over pit-falls, and mutually aiding each other to a higher outlook and firmer footing. In the ministry of loving service they are learning the process of saving their lives by losing them.

More and more that divine electricity called love is pulsating through man's nature and manifesting its redundant energy. It is overflowing the distinctions of caste, religion, nation, and race. Altruism is no longer a prosaic obligation, but an ideal privilege.

If the relentless drift is bearing away some traditional and conventional "household gods" and ecclesiastical sanctities, there is abundant compensation in the unveiling of higher ideals, the vitalizing of thought and character, and in the dispersion of rubbish which has almost hidden the divine lineaments of man's nature. Religious advancement is seen in the increased emphasis which is placed upon those living realities about which men cannot differ.